YOUR ALADDIN'S LAMP

Also by WILLIAM H. D. HORNADAY

Help for Today

Success Unlimited

Life Everlasting

By HARLAN WARE

Come, Fill the Cup (*novel*)

The Wonderful Mrs. Ingram (*novel*)

The Man on a Stick (*play—in collaboration*)

YOUR ALADDIN'S LAMP

TRUE STORIES ABOUT LIFE'S HIDDEN POWER

by William H. D. Hornaday

and Harlan Ware

SCIENCE OF MIND PUBLICATIONS

LOS ANGELES

Science of Mind Publications Edition

Third Printing June 1982

Originally published as *The Inner Light*
by Dodd, Mead & Company, New York

Published by SCIENCE OF MIND PUBLICATIONS
3251 W. Sixth Street—P.O. Box 75127
Los Angeles, California 90075

Printed in the United States of America
ISBN: 0-911336-75-3
Cover Design: Robert Allen

To Ernest—
wherever you may be—
with admiration and gratitude

Authors' Note

A parable, according to Webster, is "a short, fictitious narrative of a possible event in life or nature from which a moral or spiritual truth is drawn."

The case histories in this account of Ernest Holmes and his teaching have been presented as parables. But there is this difference: the stories were taken from the files, and though fictitious names have been used, the tales are true. In the account of *Mrs. Merey's Miracle* and in the report on *Sally Kincey,* an exception was made, and real names were used, with permission, as noted, because the changes which occurred were too remarkable to be believed if presented otherwise.

One of the authors was intimately and professionally associated with Dr. Holmes for many years. The other was his friend. From taped recordings of public lectures, from verbatim reports of seminars, and from memory, we have tried to capture the attitude and speech of a remarkable man who sought in all religions an expression of the Central Integrity in the universe.

W.H.D.H.
H.W.

Contents

YOUR ALADDIN'S LAMP

1

Mad at God

It was four o'clock. Blue sky overhead. A perfect day. As the amplifiers drenched the garden with the opening bars of Mendelssohn's Wedding March, the bride, in shimmering white—with veil—reacted convulsively in the grape arbor; and then, majestic as a sailing ship before a favoring wind, she urged her escort into the hesitant step of the processional.

The bridesmaid—and there was only one—seemed a bit distraught in pink tulle which had seen another wedding, but she quickly activated the flower girl, a starchy toddler who'd had instructions but no rehearsal. The small parade sorted itself out in proper order and moved toward the grassy aisle. The child, under orders, thrust a chubby hand into the flowery basket but failed to scatter rose petals. She'd heard a sob.

"Keep *going!*" whispered the bridesmaid fiercely.

The witnesses, in hostile clusters on either side of the

aisle, stood stiffly, looking straight ahead. Only the bride's mother glanced back at the processional. The flower girl, now being prodded from behind, moved slowly on, not so much scattering petals as placing them. Nobody beamed at her. Nobody breathed: "Isn't she cute!"

"Get *going!*"

A backward glance at the father of the bride alarmed her. She stopped abruptly. To a more sophisticated eye he would have been an obvious insurance risk, an overweight, red-faced man suffering a dangerous pressure. The child's fat fingers squeezed out a few petals. The altar where the minister, best man and bridegroom were waiting seemed very far away.

Then she glanced shyly ahead, caught a warm smile from the minister, and moved.

Diminutive in his black robe—he was five foot three—Dr. Ernest Holmes waited calmly, service book in hand. Undisturbed by what was clearly a sticky situation, he was inwardly bestowing blessings on the melancholy bridegroom, the grim best man, the glowering witnesses. Dr. Holmes was a philosopher first and a minister only when it was forced upon him, and he would approach this problem in his own unorthodox way. The challenge intrigued him. He had been born with a reverence for life, a sense of humor, and the gift of detachment. As he waited now for the dawdling flower girl to find likely spots for the petals, he studied the scene with historical perspective. It would be useful in his teaching.

The tall, quiet palm trees, not a frond stirring, placed the house on the status side of Beverly Hills. The Brown Derby caterers with their domestic champagne in shiny ice buckets were as familiar as the trees; so were the umbrellas from Abbey Rents; so were the rental chairs beside which the witnesses were standing, surely as morose a crowd as ever spoiled a wedding. None, except the mother of the bride, dared an exchange of glances. They were embarrassed, bitter, angry or sad. Now, as her son took a single step toward his approaching bride-to-be, a sob burst from the bridegroom's mother. It was as if she were in mourning. Across the aisle, her opposite number, a wrenlike matron with blue hair, was still offering pitiful, tentative smiles to anybody who might respond. Nobody responded. The witnesses were here because blood was thicker than water; they wanted nothing so much as to go home.

The flower girl and bridesmaid finally found their places. The bride and groom faced Dr. Holmes. The lifting of the needle scratched the hi-fi record; silence fell. Then there was only the pulsing hum of summer, the heavy breathing of the father of the bride, and an airplane high overhead.

Dr. Holmes waited until the last witness had creaked into the last chair. The young man reached for his bride's hand and gave it a reassuring pressure. That was nice. The girl's eyes brimmed over with gratitude. She was in her mid-twenties, a wholesome girl with a lovely complexion and he was a splendid, sea-tanned young man. There was love here. But Dr. Holmes wondered if anybody in this garden had given so much as a thought to the central element in this affair.

Friends, we are assembled here in the presence of God and these witnesses to join together this man and this woman in the bonds of holy wedlock. . . .

He was unacquainted with these people. An hour ago, at three o'clock, wearing Pendleton shirt, slacks and loafers, he had been loading books into his car in the parking lot outside the Institute in metropolitan Los Angeles. Tomorrow, and five mornings thereafter, he would lecture in the auditorium at Asilomar, a state park, about four hundred miles away, in northern California. He was to be the principal speaker at the annual Conference of Churches of Religious Science.

He heard running footsteps as he closed and locked the luggage compartment.

"Dr. Holmes j-u-s-t drove away," he said facetiously, pointing off down Sixth Street.

The secretary was not amused.

"It's an emergency," she said. "There's a desperate man on the phone. He won't hang up until he's talked to you." She added anxiously: "He's almost crying. Something awful has happened at his daughter's wedding. He wants to tell you all about it."

Emergencies were routine for Ernest Holmes. Yesterday, with an hour's notice, he had conducted a funeral for a Hebrew whose survivors couldn't agree on a rabbi. He often performed weddings for excommunicated Catholics; for Buddhists who couldn't find a temple; for Christmas Christians who had no church; for agnostics. He was no stickler for form; ecclesiasticism appealed only to his sense of humor.

He hurried back to the office, sat down in his swivel chair, glanced with a sigh at the office clock.

"What's the problem exactly?" he asked the sufferer at the other end of the line.

"You don't remember me, Dr. Holmes," the man said, unevenly, "but we shook hands once at Rotary. I'm G-G-George P. Chesney of Beverly Hills." He struggled for control. "I gotta have help right now, doctor. A fundamentalist preacher just let us down!"

"Why?"

"I wouldn't care to discuss it over the phone. Let me just say this—if we don't pull off the wedding today, we might never get another chance."

Dr. Holmes was intuitive.

"The bridegroom? Where've you got him, George?"

"Oh, he's here. The Navy flew him home from Japan. He's got three days and his travel time. Some of his relatives came up from La Jolla, too. And some of our folks are here. It's like trying to merge the Hatfields and the McCoys, though." There was a disturbance in the background; briefly he turned aside and growled: "I'm trying to tell him!" Then he was back on the line. "Y'see, my little girl Elfie always wanted a white wedding gown from Saks and that's caused some trouble because—"

A shrill detached voice told him to get to the point.

His own voice broke.

The bride was pregnant.

Not only was poor Miss Elfie Chesney pregnant; she was terminal.

And due to an anguishing delay caused by the United States Navy, and Elfie's stubbornness, and the groom's stubbornness, this ceremony had been postponed almost too long. Something might happen any minute.

Dr. Holmes took his robe, which would cover the Pendleton shirt, declined to change the loafers, sent word to his traveling companions to expect an hour's delay, and sped off toward Beverly Hills.

The Chesneys' house was a remnant of the neo-Spanish, early Hollywood era, a large house on a huge lot. The driveway had been kept open. The father of the bride rushed out to give Ernest Holmes a damp, grateful handshake. A flash of blue interrupted and the girl's mother was sobbing in his arms.

The groom turned out to be an honest young fellow who had been stationed in San Diego last year while falling in love with Elfie. When a doctor's report alarmed them both, he faced the problem squarely—but held out for a secret trip to Las Vegas and a private ceremony in a wedding chapel. Elfie, on the other hand, had dreamed of a white gown and a garden wedding all her life.

They didn't actually quarrel, but there was an impasse. Then, to their consternation, Peter had been shipped out with the fleet.

He explained:

"My mother is a highly emotional woman, Dr. Holmes. And my stepfather and I don't get along too well, so I wanted to let them meet Elfie and hear about us after Las Vegas, see? I didn't realize Elfie has a *fixation* about a white gown from Saks and a veil and a garden wedding. I gave in, of course, but then we hit the red tape. It took the Red Cross and my congressman to get me home."

He loved Elfie. And he admired her spunk. She had been soft and feminine and yielding before; but about this one dream she showed a steel spine. He called it character.

He finally wangled three days, his travel time, and a free ride in a jet. He cabled her from Kobe to select a minister.

And that's where she made her mistake.

A boy she'd known in high school had just graduated from the seminary and was assigned to his first church in a nearby suburb. She thought it would be easier with somebody she knew. The young preacher had reluctantly agreed to perform the ceremony, but his bishop, he said, was very stuffy. This morning, to protect his own position, he'd consulted the bishop, who was shocked and pointed out, with ominous severity, that white was worn to symbolize virginity. The young minister begged Elfie to wear some other color; George Chesney had lost his temper—nobody was sure now whether the minister had been fired or had quit.

Dr. Holmes was reassuring. "George," he said, "if Elfie has *affirmed* this wedding in her mind all these years, you have nothing to worry about. Nothing can stop it."

And nothing did.

The ceremony went along nicely for a paragraph or so. All was smooth as cream until Dr. Holmes reached the repetitive "before these witnesses—" He stopped abruptly.

Ernest Holmes was not only unorthodox, he was unpredictable. He trusted the Power within, the Light within. Sometimes in his Sunday sermons he betrayed astonishment when he heard himself interpreting an abstract idea in new crystal-clear phrases. Once, pausing as if listening to an echo of his own voice, he addressed the congregation with an air of honest surprise: "That *was* good, wasn't it?"

The Power within. He could always trust it.

"And before these witnesses—" he had said, and stopped.

The lengthening pause had brought a stir of apprehension. But he had not lost his place. Here was a nonconforming but reverent man; and his reverence was for God, for Life and Love. In emotion his voice took on an organ tone sometimes:

"And there is *another* witness who will be blessed by this ceremony—" he began, and shock waves washed across the garden. This wasn't done! Startled faces lifted. His manner, as he met the glances, seemed to say: Now that love, and foolishness, and stubbornness, and fear had created this dilemma, what remnant is important? He repeated: "A tiny, adorable witness who even now is responding to the love of his parents and grandparents on either side of the aisle; another witness whose life will be influenced by the friends and relatives who, after all, cared enough to come to this solemn ceremony—a ceremony which was first envisioned by a charming little girl many years ago—"

There was a creak of folding chairs, a cough; he looked up to see the mother of the bride as she won her first response: across the aisle an old man smiled, chuckled warmly, and then settled back to enjoy the wedding. The tension had broken.

From then on it was routine with congratulations, handshakes, popping of corks and, eventually, an affable blending of Hatfields and McCoys.

Dr. Holmes then sought out the bridegroom's mother, who was doing her best to brighten up, but she had further to go than most.

"They're strong young people; they'll do well," he said encouragingly.

The party gained momentum right up to the departure of the bride and groom. The bouquet was thrown rather abruptly, and the bridesmaid caught it. Rice was hurriedly distributed in small paper sacks; the guests moved en masse to the driveway. Dr. Holmes watched with the others until the fluttering white veil in the swiftly receding convertible, bound for the hospital, had disappeared in the traffic.

Then, with gaiety on all sides, he parted from his new friends and drove to the church to pick us up.

"When people forget themselves and trust the Power within," Ernest said as we drove north, "you can even bring together Hatfields and McCoys. Let me tell you what happened this afternoon. . . ."

Asilomar, toward which we were driving, had become a State Park. It offered a scattering of comfortable redwood buildings on white sand dunes on the Pacific shore at the western edge of the Monterey Peninsula. Once upon a time—through the auspices of Phoebe Apperson Hearst—it had been a summer camp for working girls; unhappily there had been no comparable nearby summer camp for working boys, and so it had languished. But now, as the property of the State of California, it had grown into a popular conference headquarters for groups who didn't require night clubs, theaters or bars. The manager once told me that his inn attracted only the type of organization whose members weren't terrified by having a quiet moment to think.

We were running late. There were wisps of fog along the seacoast, but even so, Ernest voted to take Highway #1 from San Luis Obispo—a spectacular cliffside drive five or six hundred feet above the ocean, a winding scenic highway carved from the sandstone cliffs. There'd be moonlight on the surf, a Brigadoon mistiness, a sense of adventure. Sometimes the vote was a majority of one. There were four of us in the car, but I sensed enthusiasm in only one as we left the freeway and sped along a waterfront asphalt road, gradually rising. A lighthouse sent its brazen beam across a chill, gray sea. The night turned cold. Before long we had to stop to bundle up. Then we proceeded cautiously through gathering fog.

A few miles beyond Nepenthe, in the wooded Big Sur country, our headlights picked up a lone figure at the roadside—a child, we thought at first. We saw a wistful, upraised thumb. Ernest urged a stop. It turned out to be a not very tall young man. He wore a T-shirt under a tweed jacket, and carried a small leather bag with a drawstring. He was underweight, crew-cut, horn-rimmed and, we discovered later, bright as a new penny. Ernest took him in front.

The boy was nineteen, he admitted, and would be a sophomore at Stanford next quarter, in the fall. He had hitchhiked to Los Angeles to catch a troupe of Russian dancers whom he'd missed in San Francisco. The enterprise had turned out to be unexpectedly costly. He spoke learnedly of inflation. Ernest asked if he'd had dinner; he said he had—he'd bought a banana. Soon we found that the fog was lifting and the conversation, which had centered on evidentials of healings, now turned to existentialism, communism, Freud, T. S. Eliot, Karl Marx and nihilism.

"Annihilate the idea of God or there can be no freedom," the boy told us flatly. "Annihilate civilization, property, marriage, morality and justice. Let your own happiness be the only law."

"You're pretty tweedy for a beatnik," somebody said.

"Beatniks have degraded nihilism," the boy announced. "There are no happy beatniks. They all itch."

To spare him possible embarrassment we began introductions. He was Bernard Opley of Chicago and Palo Alto, he said—and did a double-take.

"Dr. Ernest Holmes, *the minister?*" he asked, and his face froze. "A *minister!*" He was disgusted. For a moment nobody could think of anything to say.

The young fellow folded his arms and ducked his chin, ready for battle.

"I don't believe in God," he told us, and waited for a counterblow.

No counterblow. Ernest sympathized with twentieth-century young people who were unable to reconcile the old theology with the atom bomb, and space flight, the theoretical space-time continuum. He'd suffered his own adolescence in a period of change.

"You don't believe in the anthropomorphic God many people believe in," he suggested. "I don't myself."

"The Dead Sea Scrolls have blown Christianity out the window," the boy announced, and looked as if he expected somebody to scream. "There's a lot of it yet to be published, you know. Why do you suppose the churches are trying to get together? They're bracing for the storm. Much of the Sermon on the Mount appears in the scrolls—*and they're dated two hundred years before Jesus.* There goes the Virgin Mary. That's the end of the Nicene Creed, the Trinity and the Holy Ghost. The church isn't alive, sir; it's dead and merely twitching. What have you got left?"

"Well," Ernest said mildly, "it seems to me we have the Christ Consciousness. It has never been affected by conventions of bishops, and we have the great Jesus of Nazareth and his demonstration that the Christ Consciousness has always been in the world, and always will be. Nothing has ever excelled his manifestation of it."

"You will pardon me, Dr. Holmes, but I think that's eyewash. I don't believe in any God whatever. It's a mechanistic universe."

"Well, now," Ernest said, smiling. "Can you prove it?"

The young voice took on emotion:

"After Buchenwald and Dachau and wholesale murders of millions in Russia and China, and the starvation right now in Asia, it ought to be pretty obvious what kind of a world it is. For billions of people it's anguish with the gods left out."

"Have you ever attended a church?"

"Wow! *Have* I!" He turned in the seat, half facing Ernest. "Doctor, when I was a little boy, four years old maybe—so young that when I sat in a pew my feet wouldn't touch the floor—I remember the preacher pouring out sermons like so much hot lava—and I swung my legs and thought: *None of this is true!* I couldn't say that to my folks, of course, or to anybody, but even then I knew none of it is true."

"Hellfire and brimstone, was it?"

"You betcha. Original sin. I was born rotten, the preacher said. Only way to turn myself inside out, and avoid hell, was to grovel at his feet and pray and get there on time Sundays with my dime. His preaching sure worried some of the little kids, but it never worried me."

"At *four?*"

"Well, five, maybe—but it was before I went to public school. When I did get to school, I talked it over with the older boys and they didn't believe it either. Then I found out my folks didn't actually believe it; they said it was a way to think on Sundays. It was moral training.

"Well, one Sunday morning when I was about eight, a beautiful spring day, I was walking home and I could smell lilacs, and I said to God: 'Look, You. If You're as mean as our preacher says You are—*strike me down!'* I stood in the middle of the sidewalk, looking up, with my arms spread, waiting."

"Brave lad."

"Yeah, I sure was. There was water running in the gutters from an early rain, and a sparkle over everything and a deep blue sky without a lightning bolt in it; not even thunder. I walked home on top o' the world; I've been free ever since."

Ernest listened attentively and then asked: "By the way, I have a special fund for agnostics under twenty. How'd you like to be my guest at Asilomar and eat a few square meals?"

The boy turned instantly suspicious. He grunted something negative and dropped into a brooding silence. Ernest hooked his arm on the back of the seat and looked around at the rest of us.

"Ecclesiasticism," he murmured. "Y'see? It's wrecking religion."

Bernard bristled. "But I never had a religion, and I'm doing fine without it. I got all A's last year."

"Where'd you go to high school?"

"New Trier, that's outside of Chicago. It's at Winnetka, Illinois, a suburb."

"How'd you get along?"

"I was a Merit Scholar."

"It's the bright ones they lose first," Ernest told us, "and then they lose the others later on. It isn't the fault of all those good-hearted preachers, either. It's the old theology. Bernard?"

"Sir?"

"There will be young people at Asilomar who have been mad at God. You'll enjoy it."

"Why the sales talk?"

"Because I've met you before somewhere."

"You're mistaken, sir."

"It doesn't matter. You're invited. Take it or leave it."

Bernard was tempted. There were still patches of fog. And it was getting on toward midnight.

"I might stay tonight, anyhow."

Nobody congratulated him.

As we approached the great redwood gates at Asilomar, he said:

"Why would you care what *I* think, Dr. Holmes?"

Ernest grinned. "I just like to keep abreast of current trends."

Later, when we registered at the desk in the Administration Building, Ernest drew me aside.

"That's a good boy. He's hiding his charm, I'll admit, but I know the type pretty well." He lifted his voice and waggled a finger. "Bernard! You and Dr. Hornaday should have much in common. He was a rebel once, too. He went to China with plans to become a missionary—and found out the heathen he'd come to save knew more about religion than he did."

Bernard reacted as if "missionary" were one of the most distasteful words in the English language. Only the eyes of youth can deliver such wounding looks.

"Among other things," I said, into that fixed stare of rejection which is so familiar in classrooms, "I learned that the Chinese had known about psychosomatic medicine about four thousand years before we heard about it."

"Our agnostic looks as if he could use a sandwich," Ernest suggested. "What do you weigh, Bernard?"

"I'm down right now," the boy admitted. "I've done lots of walking on this trip, and I've had a cold."

"How tall?"

Bernard stood straight. "Well, I'm still growing, sir."

"Taller than I am, at that," Ernest mused.

There were college men Bernard's age in one of the hilltop dormitories and snacks were available. After the introductions Bernard followed me out the door.

"What does Dr. Holmes really want of me?" he demanded. "Is he saving souls, or what?"

"He's after material, I imagine."

"Sir?"

"He'll deliver five lectures before the week is out. He wants to know if the thinking of young people has changed lately."

Bernard gave me a bleak smile.

"I'm hungry enough to talk to a Holy Roller," he admitted. "Good night."

Monterey Peninsula is cool, sometimes downright cold, in summer, and the fireplaces were welcome. Nowadays when I think of Asilomar, there's a memory of fragrant wood smoke drifting through pine trees on the fresh sea air. Ernest's favorite cottage was near the lecture hall, put down amid dwarf cypress not far from the long rocky beach. The living room, looking out on dunes which funneled to the sea, boasted a big fireplace and comfortable armchairs.

After the lectures Ernest often invited a few potential critics in for coffee. "Did you understand what I was saying this morning?" he once asked a group of new students. Everybody had. "Good," he said happily. "Explain it to me, then. There was a lot of it I didn't understand myself."

He always insisted he'd never had a revelation, yet when the creative obsession was upon him, there were times when his lecture could best be described with the embarrassing word "illumined."

In rereading my notes for that first morning, it is obvious that his encounter with Bernard had provided a springboard for the first lecture. After the opening remarks I remember looking around for the boy. It was a relief to find him there. He sat on a straight chair, tilted back against the far wall, watching the sturdy short figure at the podium with scornful, half-closed eyes.

Ernest, when teaching, rarely lectured without a blackboard; indeed, he used blackboards sometimes in church. His approach to religion was like Einstein's—thoughts go into formulae and shake the world.

That morning he wore a sports shirt I'd never seen before, probably purchased for the occasion. Nobody would have taken him for a cleric—not even for a cleric on holiday.

On that particular morning he said:

"A great many people have a big superiority complex, which is merely an inferiority complex whistling to keep up its courage!

"A boy once asked me what I did. I told the boy that I was a certain kind of minister and he asked what kind. I told him that I didn't like any of the religions I was acquainted with and so I had made up one that I did like. He thought that was crazy, and it does sound that way, but if you studied history, you would find that this is the way all religions are founded. Each is just a new version of the old, and people will call the new one 'odd' for a while, like a new style, but by and by everyone accepts it.

"This is literally true. This is the way all of our religions or theologies have been started. This is the way we get our words; somebody has to make them up. God doesn't have a fountain pen and write in a ledger and drop the leaves of it on the hilltop!

"We say that the mountains show forth the glory of God, but it isn't that way. The mountains *are* the glory of God in the same sense that Einstein's second equation tells us that energy and mass are equal, identical and interchangeable. This equation is fundamental to our philosophy, for Einstein isn't saying that energy energizes mass. That is exactly what he isn't saying. He is not saying that it flows through and influences and controls mass. He says energy *is* mass. Spinoza said, 'Mind and matter are the same thing.' Now modern physics is beginning to tell us that the physical universe is but a shadow of some substance which we do not see.

"These mountains here do not reflect the glory of God, they *are* the glory of God. In other words, there isn't a mountain which God 'up there' reflects into a mirror so that we see a mountain 'down here.' The mountain is God's idea of Himself that way. That is why we can commune with nature in her visible form, and that is why a tree can speak to us, which it most certainly can, if we would develop the ability to listen." *

There were two hundred people in the audience that morning, and many of them crowded up to the platform. Bernard was not among them.

* From Seminar Lectures.

"I hear there are some good trails down to the beach," he said pointedly. "If it's a warm day tomorrow, I might miss the lecture, Dr. Hornaday."

"But if you get cold, come back," I said. "We keep this room rather cozy."

Ernest joined us.

"Bernard, what did you get out of what I just said?" he asked.

"Nothing," said our guest promptly. "It sounded like so much mishmash to me, sir."

Everyone within earshot bristled, but the atmosphere was immediately brightened by Ernest's beaming smile.

"How're your politics?"

"Communism doesn't scare me, if that's what you're fishing for," the boy said.

"I knew it wouldn't," Ernest said, nodding.

He suggested lunch and we moved to a table in the commissary. Ernest placed Bernard at his right but addressed two very pretty girls who sat across the table.

"In these days," he said, as we all proceeded to eat a farm-type lunch, the sort called for in that crisp, cool weather, "a young man's caustic attitude toward what he calls religion, and which is actually the old theology, isn't unreasonable.

"To frustrate growth by an insistence on rusty forms and superstitious beliefs is to tarnish the light he brought into the world. In the age of the atom, supersonic flight, television, fabulous experiments in ESP—and documented discoveries—an insistence on an angry Jehovah on a throne in the skies, will frustrate genius, frighten children and make disbelievers of our brightest young men and women. Some theology-ridden, well-intentioned preacher, hammering away on outmoded dogmas, will drive them out of the churches and onto the highways, where they'll hold up a thumb, boast of their agnosticism and scorn God."

Bernard was sitting straight up. He hadn't heard much of that which had been said—listened, perhaps, as if it had been a college lecture—but he felt that the time had come for debate. He put down his fork.

"How did your good God allow that slaughter in the Nazi ovens?" he demanded, planting both hands on his knees, elbows up. "Or the starvation of the Russian peasants by the million under Stalin? You don't answer these questions, sir. How could any God worth knowing permit the cruelty of man to man down through the ages?"

Ernest asked, gently:

"Bernard, have you any quarrel with the orderly stars? Or the dependable tides? With the warmth of the sun, the change in seasons, the beauty of nature, the intelligence and thrust in seed and soil? Any quarrel with your own ability to think your way in and out of corners? Why, the conveying of ideas to one another, sometimes without words, sometimes at a distance, having *awareness* in this world of dazzling beauty, what is that but God, nearer than breathing, closer than hands and feet?

"We affirm a belief in a universe of ultimate good because we, too, have doubted, questioned, explored—and now have a backlog of case histories. You'll only know that I speak the truth when you have proof of your own. Then you may arrive at the reassuring notion that an instant expansion in your thinking—a technique which will lift you from where you are and give you the view from a tower—can dissolve your problems. We are carrying on this amiable discussion on a planet which moves with predictable precision amid stars which have existed for uncountable years, for an eternity, open at both ends; because if there is no end, there was no beginning, and we've got to stretch our concepts for another view of Time."

"You've been talking about impersonal, physical laws, Dr. Holmes. In a good universe." Bernard pointed toward the sea. "But if I walk out into that dependable tide and can't swim, I'll drown."

"That's right. And the incoming surf will be as beautiful as ever."

"But where's your good God in that?"

"Where He has always been—expressing Infinite Wisdom! He is forever the Light within a universe of achieved perfection—within which there is a dimension with plenty of room for the evolving soul of Bernard Opley."

"But I'm dead. I just drowned."

"You still have the greatest gifts ever bestowed: consciousness and free will. You simply start over."

"Theory!" Bernard hammered the table. "Look, if I'd been at Buchenwald, that impersonal God of yours would have let me die along with millions of others in the worst savagery ever known to man."

"You haven't outgrown the church at home, Bernard," Ernest said sharply. "The God you don't believe in is an anthropomorphic concept, and gone with the wind. I wouldn't want to know a God who can tell the difference between Jew, Gentile, Catholic, Protestant, black, white, red, brown or yellow. Consciousness has no color and no creed. No sane man in these days would acknowledge a God who might suspend cosmic laws in special instances; yet if you'll *search,* your own expanding awareness will lead you to discover laws that supersede laws, and your *understanding* of this might very well have led to your escape."

"This is utter and absolute mishmash!" Bernard said. "I haven't the faintest idea what you're saying."

Ernest sighed.

"Here's an illustration borrowed from Thomas Troward," he said. "Listen carefully now; for centuries man accepted this as law: a bar of iron placed in water will sink. Nobody doubted this. Everybody could prove it. But it was not the truth, the whole truth. That law is superseded by another—and iron will float. Heat it, shape it, close the ends, displace water with it and it becomes an iron ship. As your studies take you in this direction, you keep discovering laws superseding other laws, then you find the *technique* so that you may function comfortably in such a universe—and what happens then will sometimes seem miraculous."

After two attempts Bernard met the wry, smiling glance of a girl across the aisle.

"That argument about one law superseding another isn't too terrible, at that," Bernard said, and subsided.

Later we watched him walking toward the beach with the girl, and Ernest said warmly:

"Awful nice kid, Bill. But I wouldn't want to be nineteen again, would you?"

At nineteen, what had I been doing, thinking? I had been playing the marimba in a dance band but planning to become a missionary—and how was that for mixed-up?

"There's no telling what will happen to these young people when they begin to recognize the Power within," Ernest said, but he sighed. "No lecture ever reaches them, I suppose."

That evening we were lingering over coffee at the big table when someone sharply challenged us. Bernard had pointedly avoided our table but sat within earshot: before long he had pulled up a chair.

In a book called *Help for Today,* Ernest Holmes and I had written the line: "Prayer is not an Aladdin's lamp."

That evening our critic said:

"There's a deeper meaning in the old fairy tale which the average reader misses."

Somebody else remembered that I had preached a sermon about Aladdin's lamp at the Wiltern Theater, probably about eleven years ago.

This had been the stirring of an idea never fully explored. The men and women at the table that evening, an editor, a writer, several practitioners and ministers, had wrought miracles in their own lives with Religious Science—almost like receiving help from a genie—and the metaphysical aspects of the Aladdin lamp story fired their imaginations.

"There's truth in fiction," our critic went on. "Any tale that survives the ages must convey a basic truth. The legend of Aladdin and his wonderful lamp was kept alive by word of mouth for centuries before it first saw print in 1710."

He sketched the story for those who had forgotten the details. The essentials were these:

When the fifteen-year-old boy Aladdin, up to then a ne'er-do-well, acquired the tarnished lamp after much difficulty, his mother decided to sell it to buy food, for they were very poor. Aladdin's father, Mustapha the tailor, had died of a broken heart because the boy roamed the streets and wouldn't work—he had been a juvenile delinquent long before the phrase was coined. The overworked mother, unaware that the lamp had special properties, began to rub off the tarnish, and *poof!* a genie appeared, a spirit-slave who could instantly produce miracles of abundance. And did. Aladdin became a wealthy and respected citizen, generous to the poor. He acquired castles and a princess—and the tale was one of worldly riches won and lost and won again.

One early scholar researching the story had concluded: It has no religious significance.

But what of the metaphysical symbolism?

The Light that Lighteth every man who comes into the world?

The word *genie* could be traced to the word *genius.*

Wasn't there, after all, a powerful metaphysical truth hidden here? Was abundance the least of it?

Did the tale say: Each man is an Aladdin, sometimes unaware of his power, but possessed of the Light that Lighteth every man—

Possessed of genius?

Every man's genius?

Was the story telling us a truth we instinctively recognized: that any man could know health, abundance, peace of mind and heart, by turning to the Power within? The *I* within. The Light which was his own awareness, his own consciousness?

Each of us could trust to the Power within when rightly understood and disciplined; was that it?

The genie was everyman's genius; thus, it might be said to each of us: *Rub that lamp, Aladdin!*

We surveyed the towering talents which had visited this planet, men and women who moved beyond self-imposed limitations and found the true illumination which produced Shakespeare's plays and sonnets, and Bacon's essays, and Plato's philosophy, Beethoven's symphonies, Da Vinci's "Last Supper." There had been a shining glory of expression all down through time. Any modern creative artist could testify to his own experience when, thrusting beyond self-consciousness, the creative channels suddenly opened and the flow came free. Writers, painters, composers, inventors—and not these alone, but also agriculturists, businessmen, scholars—all creative people discovered in the deep self a mind that was forever creating, forever renewing.

And it was forever yours. And forever mine.

There was a way open to all men.

A parable in the form of a children's fairy tale had brought down through the centuries a profound truth for those who took the pains to find it.

There were techniques which all might use.

There was a lamp, and a genie, a way to a richer life of the Spirit.

Here was a realm which the physical scientists had pointedly ignored, we said. Mighty intellects had explored the physical universe with such skill, such genius, that it led to the discovery of a bomb which would burn this lovely earth to a cinder. But the realm of the spirit had been left to the theologians.

And as Ben Franklin said:

> Many a long dispute among Divines may be thus abridged;
> It is so; it is not so. It is so; it is not so.

If man's genius had taken him so far into the physical universe that, now, he could blow himself out of the skies, it was time for genius to ignore impractical creeds and dogmas and hasten in the opposite direction. The same enterprise and dedication would discover a spiritual realm so vast and so reassuring as to dwarf all other achievements.

The students of Science of Mind could present, for the examination of the skeptic, case histories by the score.

Conviction lay in demonstration, of course; and more records should be gathered, Ernest said, and presented in readable fashion . . . for not every agnostic cared to embrace the empty darkness of his tomb; the void was so appalling many would explore a path that looked reasonable. The old theology wasn't reasonable, that was all.

"I know a man, a celebrated actor, who long ago lost all sense of religion," Ernest told us, "but the other night, as he was leaving my house, he said wistfully, 'We sure need *something.*' "

The actor had sent Ernest an autobiography in which there appeared a paragraph he wanted us to hear. We left the dining hall and drifted into the living room at Tide Inn, where a pine log fire was crackling on the hearth.

Before long I noticed Bernard and a pretty brunette sitting on the floor with their backs against the wall. They were politely silent but not attentive, I thought, and so dismissed them.

"Let me read you one paragraph," Ernest begged, thumbing through the book. "This is a classic excursion into autobiography by J. B. Priestley, called *Midnight on the Desert.* I've enjoyed it immensely." He looked up. "And Mr. Priestley often uses the lamp most effectively himself." He found his place. "Now, defending his interest in a theory of Time, which is anything but naive, Priestley says:

"Apparently, I could not resist running up and down the sixth dimension. If there was one, and this was not all moonshine. But, why, I said to myself, should I not believe in this enchanting universe of many dimensions, in which we shall come at last, after much conflict and sorrow, to work everything out right, as we do in our novels and plays? If some of my friends speak the truth when they tell me we exist only for a brief period, reproduce our kind, and are obliterated by death, then it only means that one night I shall go to bed still exploring this enchanting universe of many dimensions, then fall asleep in it forever. If they are right, I shall not wake from that sleep to go exploring my universe, but I shall never know that they were right and I was wrong, and during my midget life under the sun, I shall have known a better universe than they do or than nature and reality know how to make. Give me my robe, put on my crown, I have immortal longings in me." *

So it was with Ernest. He had immortal longings in him. But more: he was convinced that the mechanists were wrong.

He believed in the survival of consciousness.

He believed in immortality.

He believed that Jesus of Nazareth, when honestly reported, meant exactly what he said.

And it didn't matter if the Dead Sea Scrolls had turned up the Sermon on the Mount in an Essene monastery two hundred years earlier. The Christ Consciousness as expressed by Jesus had altered history, lifted mankind, and given hope to the world. Jesus had understood the Power within, the Father within, and had expressed the concept

* From *Midnight on the Desert,* by J. B. Priestley, Harper & Bros. Copyright 1937.

in words that had never been improved upon, and never forgotten.

That was the evening that Ernest Holmes, a lifetime student of all religions, said with such conviction that no one could doubt his sincerity, that he and his beloved wife Hazel and his old dog Prince would meet again.

"Prince has a discreet bark, just for me," he said, "and I'll hear it. And Hazel will be waiting in some dimension I can't envision now—but there they'll be."

The fire crackled in the room's warm silence and I thought of what he had said in the lecture that morning:

"What the average man means when he says he doesn't believe in God is that he doesn't believe in immortality."

His own belief was a reassurance, a glimpse down an endless corridor where far away and in the mists all his true loves were ready to welcome him. And that he did truly believe, this I know—because I was with him on that last day when it was tested.

He walked out with me that evening when everyone else had gone. He loved the view at any hour, but especially when the evening silence came. From where we were standing, dwarf cypress trees made a soft, green, low-growing accent against the white sand. He enjoyed walking to the top of the highest dune to watch the cresting waves in the moonlight. At certain daylight hours there was a color, an aquamarine, to be seen in the rays of the sun; it was caught in the underside of the wave and was almost unbearably beautiful.

That evening, leaving him at Tide Inn, I knew that his thoughts went with us after we had said good night; he is gone now, and the months and the years are passing, but the warmth of the man is with us still.

2

Mental Health Bread

With faith smaller than a mustard seed, combined with the techniques in Ernest Holmes' philosophy, we bought a house in Carmel which was not for sale with the profits from a house in the smog which could not be sold.

This testimony comes from the co-author of this effort (who will now briefly assume the first person) and the evidential will be offered in its proper place. To certain startled witnesses a mountain had moved. A friend told Hazel Holmes about it and Hazel told Ernest.

"And the people who bought the house in the smog?" Ernest inquired mildly. "How do *they* like it?"

"Papa, that's the astonishing part!" Hazel reassured him. "Everybody got what he wanted. There are Californians who actually rather like smog for reasons of their own. After the morning lecture we're going to Carmel for lunch to hear all about it."

We always called Hazel Madame Buddha. She was serene. Peace was everywhere around her, as if she moved in the eye of the hurricane; you could sit down nearby and rest. Writers especially were soothed by her composure Papa was a creative person, too, as she said, and she made the weather for him. She made a climate for everybody. The first time I ever saw her she gave me a dozen usable ideas which at that moment lulled the winds of apprehen sion.

This was 1955, during the seminar—long before the incidents in our opening chapter—and in that period my well-oiled Remington was producing fifteen thousand words every week for Carlton E. Morse's *One Man's Family,* a radio show which had been on the air for two decades. My wife Ruthie—known to certain lady golfers as "poor Ruthie"—was attached to her electric typewriter on a long golden chain. When I had completed the day's work begun at four o'clock in the morning—that blessed hour when the citizens who create the turmoil are still having their nightmares and a lovely world belongs to those who go to bed at eight—Ruthie would be hauled in like a flounder from wherever she happened to be. When I was desperately behind schedule, a caddy could be seen loping across the beautiful scenery near the sixteenth at Pebble Beach.

Too often it was a near-thing. We finally discovered a back road to the airport and often handed aboard the last plane a script due in Hollywood in the morning. It would have been a splendid way of life for the young; but we'd been free lancing for twenty-five years, living, in Ralph Bellamy's phrase, from hand to mouth in a big way. Happy but heedless. And a morning came, after novels, essays, screen plays, short stories, radio shows, articles, when there was nothing in my head but sand.

Someone recommended Ernest Holmes' books *Creative Mind* and *Creative Mind and Success.* Finding Ernest was like finding a faucet. The well filled up, the flow of ideas returned. I wrote him a fan letter which can be summed up in two words: *Saved again.*

Thus began the friendship. But Ruth hadn't met Ernest that first day in Carmel, when they came to lunch. A large car pulled up at the gate at exactly twelve-thirty and there he was, all five foot three of him back of the wheel, wearing his Pendelton shirt. Hazel was smartly turned out, as always, in a tweed suit with hat, furs and gloves.

"And he's a *minister?*" Ruth whispered to me as we went to greet them.

I told them what Ruth had said. Ernest was delighted. He had been known to go to extremes to keep from being labeled an ecclesiastic.

The Institute of Religious Science and Philosophy had been founded because he was a teacher with a new expression of a profound idea, and he had lectured, and written his many books to bind the message; but he never really wanted a church and wasn't interested in church organization. When, under the leadership of my collaborator, Dr. William H. D. Hornaday, the magnificent Founder's Church in metropolitan Los Angeles was built, Ernest was pleased to find the sixteen hundred seats filled twice each Sunday morning, and he even, grudgingly, came to admire the choir. But he had never cared for choirs, soloists or flowers in front of the lectern. When he lectured at the theater, he used to say: "The lecture is the thing."

The point is made clear for posterity in color movies taken while the church was being built. It is a graceful structure, designed by Paul R. Williams, modern as tomorrow, but as the work progresses, Ernest walks through the color film like a mildly interested sidewalk superintendent with something else on his mind. The films show scenes of general enthusiasm after the church was finished but now Ernest is discovered wandering around like a man waiting for a bus. And, by then, he *was* waiting for a bus. He had spent a scholarly lifetime searching the world's religions for a central factor, had found it, proved it out to his own satisfaction, and was ready to extend the exploration. He was lonely. Hazel was gone.

But back there at the 1955 seminar she was very much with us and our first luncheons were a riotous success; Ernest was a raconteur with a bagful of stories which nobody had ever heard, most of which had actually happened. Then, too, there was poor Ruthie's homemade bread—which we called "mental health bread." The recipe had come to us from a New York publisher after his recovery from a nervous breakdown. To our delight, and over Hazel's protest, Ernest insisted on returning the next noon with a group of editors, practitioners and ministers. He wanted certain people to get acquainted with homemade bread which had been kneaded with vigor by a writer trying to rid himself of aggressions.

The next day Ernest remarked to a thin, wiry lady minister from the north:

"When people diet, the first thing they give up is the staff of life. How long since you've had a slice of homemade bread?"

The recipe called for unbleached flour, lard—not a substitute—honey instead of sugar, and one or two other secret ingredients known to pioneers. It was so good it made some people cry. And it was baked just prior to the guests' arrival so that the fragrance lingering in the house carried the lucky ones back to childhood. Small individual loaves, with individual cutting boards and knives, and sweet butter were at each plate at a long table. In addition to the bread there was, always, a sturdy French soup and wine. Ernest pointedly accepted a glass of wine. One. No more. We weren't even sure he liked it. But he always lifted his glass ceremoniously to toast the occasion.

"Tell the folks the story behind this mental health bread," he would say, sawing away at his loaf. "My, my"—with a glance at Hazel—"it's been a long time since I've had homemade bread."

She always smiled serenely and said something to make him laugh.

He invited us to the Asilomar lectures, and if we went the first time in politeness, we returned daily as students. It was fascinating to watch Ernest detach himself from his eloquence, listen to it, comment on it. Here at the conference he was among his own people; he could let himself soar. He ad-libbed, we suspected, until he had found a theme to his liking; then a creative obsession took over and he spoke in polished paragraphs which might have gone right into print.

This is how genius works. Metaphysical abstractions would be brilliantly clarified as he sketched formulas on the blackboard; poetry, out of a vast remembering, would come gracefully to sum up his theme. He was sensitive to the point of prescience; about the time the listener was growing aware of the eloquence, Ernest would twist out of it with a flash of pixie humor. It was like hearing a glass crash backstage. *Crash—bang!* Then everybody came back to earth in a free fall from outer space.

Once a lady praised him too extravagantly while his eyes still held the gleam of concentration; he emerged abruptly.

"Thanks for the taffy," he said tartly. And then, fearing that he'd hurt her, he added soothingly: "That's all right. I'd rather have a little taffy now than a lot of epitaphy later."

He had a twinkling respect for puns. But he was scholar, writer, lecturer, founder of a church which was integrated long before the word hit the headlines; a lovable, life-adoring, witty, sensible, vastly intelligent, kindly, convinced man—and how's that for taffy, Ernest?

When he came to luncheons after Hazel had gone into what he referred to as "another expression," there was the pattern as before but not the gaiety. Other people were obliged to tell the stories now.

In other years Ernest had told an anecdote about a Hollywood garden wedding for which the father of the bride had engaged a symphony orchestra to play the wedding march while a blimp circled overhead dropping five-pound packages of rose petals. Unhappily the rose petals had congealed and failed to separate. Instead of fluttering down like rosy snow in a beautiful special Technicolor effect, they came thudding downward in solid squares and only broke apart when they struck something. The blimp, unaware of the disaster, made two passes, and then added a final treetop third for good measure. It was fifteen minutes before the guests and musicians could be rounded up. The conductor and kettledrummer, former GI's, were located in a ditch across the road. Somebody said they'd dug it.

The story as Ernest told it was so funny that once a minister from San Diego fell right off his chair; and I happen to know that Bill Hornaday can't get through it—he breaks down and cries.

That last day I thought laughter would be good for Ernest, and since we had some new auditors, urged him to tell the rose petal story. "Oh, everybody's heard that one," he said.

He had arrived with the usual entourage, but he looked lonely. As we crossed the patio, he stopped suddenly. He assured us that he'd heard a camellia sobbing, "I'm thirsty!" And he was right. Dry as desert sand. While he was busy watering every potted plant in the patio, I noticed amid the group a whey-faced, crew-cut, horn-rimmed boy who looked as if he yearned to be elsewhere.

"This is my young nonbelieving friend Bernard Opley," Ernest said warmly, after the hose had been put away. "He's one of the few American agnostics who's really working at it. He's sending a petition to Congress requesting that IN GOD WE TRUST be taken off our coins and currency. Show the folks the petition, Bernard."

The boy sent it around nervously, keeping a wary eye on Ernest. There were a few immature signatures under an impassioned paragraph urging Congress to remove "that quaint old phrase IN GOD WE TRUST from the nation's money in the name of twentieth-century common sense." The phrase was, the petitioners said, undemocratic; it put unbelievers in a false position; it was grossly unfair to the intellectuals. Men and women like the petitioner, who didn't trust God for a minute, were obliged to subscribe to a falsehood whenever they spent or earned fifty cents or a dollar.

"Why, it's naive!" Bernard insisted. "It's Boy Scout stuff."

"You don't approve of the Boy Scouts?"

He flushed angrily, folded his arms and summed it all up:

"It's—it's *square!*"

Ernest examined the word with a philologist's skill. In the slang of his own youth, "square" meant: upright, honorable, forthright, dependable, kind, generous. In a weird reversal of social standards these characteristics were now objectionable to the young.

"If you're going to talk about *ethics,*" Bernard said loftily, "the slogan is a lie. If we really trusted God, would we need an army, navy, air force or the atom bomb? I'm for realism!"

It was a crusher; he was content.

Ernest, chuckling, invited him inside the house to the west window for the view of Pt. Lobos, Carmel River and the bay, a marine landscape which had attracted us to the house when it wasn't for sale.

"A spectacular cosmic accident," Ernest suggested drily. "It produced white sand, dwarf cypress, blue sea and all those graceful coves. Remarkable that out of a senseless, tumbling explosion such incredible beauty should come, um? Did you know that the winter tides take the white sand from Carmel beach and the rough gravel from other nearby beaches, hold it until spring and then return it? The fine white sand goes back to the Carmel beach, and the gravel to the rougher beaches. It's never been known to make a mistake, either. What law of chance is operating here, I wonder?" He regarded Bernard with a brooding, sympathetic eye and then brightened at once when lunch was announced.

The bread recipe had evolved somewhat by now. A cup

of cornmeal and blackstrap molasses had been added, and the bread was better than ever. On a Saturday wine tour Ruthie and I had found, only forty miles from home, a hidden-away, little-known winery which produced two superb table wines which, when decanted and bottled in our own cellar, matched anything under labels and cost a fraction as much.

"An aspect of abundance I hadn't considered," Ernest said. He began to look happier as he wielded the bread knife. "And now, once again, please, for the people who haven't heard it, the yarn about the publisher's mental health bread. Now, listen to this, Bernard. You're building up aggressions, and here's a cure."

An engaging, personable and highly civilized New York publisher had ventured too far from Park Avenue, Twenty-One, the Stork and Scarsdale; one Monday morning he found himself married to his fifth wife, a charming and successful lady writer who owned a desert ranch on the Mojave which boasted an adobe house, an artesian well, fresh air, thirty-five unobstructed miles of scenery, and utter, breathless quiet.

However, the publisher was accustomed to noise, confusion, carbon monoxide and publication-day martinis. The silence and fresh air unsettled him, and before long his reason tottered. Maggie, his bride, rushed him to a sanitarium in the Sierra Madre foothills. We were living nearby at the time in the house that couldn't be sold. She phoned us in great distress from the sanitarium and presently she started out through the heavy smog to find us.

Only the day before a large FOR SALE sign had been placed on our front lawn by a realty company. We told her to watch for this. But she got lost. The subdivision property originally had been one of the early California ranchos, level forest land covered with live oaks; but the oaks were blighted now in the smog, and many another ranch-type house also bristled with FOR SALE signs.

"You'll never sell this white elephant with all those other white elephants being offered," Maggie said, her eyes streaming, when she finally arrived. "I'm so used to good air I can't bear it. But Sam doesn't mind it at all. He likes smog!"

Sam was her husband—Sam Dubois, we'll call him.

"We're not going to be discouraged," Ruth said, bringing in the tea things. "We've had two prospects already. We're approaching this in a little different fashion."

She didn't tell Maggie about Ernest Holmes and the Science of Mind techniques for fear of being relegated to the lunatic fringe—though, of course, Maggie at this juncture was in no position to lord it over anybody.

"Sam's terribly jumpy, but they'll let him have visitors in a week or so," she said, nervously gulping hot tea. "The doctor plans to have him kneading bread soon and that *always* calms them down."

"What?"

"Oh, yes," she said brightly, turning to me. "Did you ever hear of a pioneer wife with a nervous breakdown?"

"Now that you bring it up, I never did."

"You see! They got rid of their aggressions by kneading dough. Oh, yes, now, don't look so skeptical. The doctor has done a *paper* on it for a medical journal. He has cured hundreds of writers and actors and people like that, and editors."

"What did Sam do, exactly, Maggie?"

"Oh, *dear!*" she cried. "It was frightening! I knew he

was nervous, but I had no *idea!* One day he picked up *my* typewriter—we've been working in the same studio, y'know—and threw it out the window, and then he went around like a vandal, smashing everything I owned."

It was very sad. In a profession in which, by rote and rule, unstable characters chisel mist, spin cobwebs and make substance out of nothing, as I once pointed out in an essay, the nervous breakdown is regarded with utmost sympathy. We agreed to phone the psychiatrist and pay Sam a visit as soon as possible.

In midafternoon a couple of weeks later, we were ushered into the sunny kitchens of that handsome hilltop sanitarium. Sam Dubois was in white apron and chef's bonnet working at a butcher's table. He glowed with stability. His fingernails had been scrubbed like a surgeon's and his attire was spotless. With a heavy rolling pin he was belaboring a great head-shaped mound of yeasty resistant dough. After a series of tremendous whacks he pummeled it with his fists, glancing sometimes at the clock.

"Hi, sweethearts," he said, gloriously happy. "It's a magnificent therapy! You think about what bothers you, and the next thing you know, you've kneaded for twenty minutes and the texture is oily outside and silky within. Look!"

He'd been making ten loaves a day for a week now, he said, and sleeping at night like a baby.

"What do you think about, for instance, Sam, while you're whacking?"

"Well," he said, shaping the dough again into forehead and ears, "do you remember a writer named so-and-so? The stinker gouged me for three big advances and now he's given up writing, moved to Spain and decided to *paint!*"

The doughy head looked very much like so-and-so by now. Up went the rolling pin, and *wham.*

But laughter brimmed in Sam's eyes; we decided we were being kidded. Grover Jones, the screen writer, used to say that everybody knows his own business, plus writing; in these days it is equally true that everybody knows his own business, plus psychiatry. On the way home we diagnosed Sam's trouble: the upset had not been caused by the author who owed him money. Sam had acquired too many wound units without enough balancing ego points. Nothing brings on a nervous breakdown quicker than loss of self-esteem.

In the peace and quiet and fresh air of his wife's desert sanctuary, Sam had written a book. He had always planned to write a book and show his authors how it was done, when he "had time to sit down." And out on the pulsing Mojave he had the time and he did sit down. His own firm had printed it on good paper and launched it in champagne. And he had thrown his wife's typewriter out the window after reading the New York reviews.

Newspapers turn yellow, are collected by Boy Scouts, and time heals wounds. Sam recovered, divorced Maggie, and wrote us a pleasant little note from Scarsdale, along with the recipe. Under "Kneading" he had written:

> Knead with fists or rolling pin with great vigor for at least twenty minutes. This will relieve your aggressions. At the point where your troubles become uproariously funny the cure begins. But the best bread is kneaded with love.

Ernest recommended bread-making to one of his editors, who was biting through the cellophane on a package of cigarettes and then, putting down his napkin, he turned a thoughtful eye on Bernard. The boy had worked his way enthusiastically to the heel of the loaf, but now he grew wary in the silence.

"Bernard," Ernest asked gently, "have you ever studied the nation's annual budget?"

"No, sir."

"How big is the national debt; do you know?"

Bernard put down his knife.

"No, sir."

"Ever see the Leaning Tower of Pisa?"

"No, sir."

"Son, I'm personally acquainted with businessmen who go to Washington occasionally and come away terrified. They can't figure out what holds it all together. Can you account for it?"

Bernard shrugged.

"M'boy, in gratitude for this excellent luncheon I want to offer a primary lesson in the techniques of my philosophy. Will you hold still for it?"

"Yes, sir, Dr. Holmes."

"Now, this philosophy is *derived.* I never had a revelation, final or otherwise, and the knowledge I've acquired was here on earth when I arrived and will still be available after I've shuffled off. Whenever you find *truth,* it belongs to everybody. You can't patent or copyright it. Truth isn't a product of our thinking. It exists. Now I'll not ask anyone to accept this, but I must begin with a central assumption: nothing but good is going on."

Bernard drew a deep breath.

"The assumption can be debated later," Ernest continued, "but of this I, myself, am convinced: out there in the vast reaches of outer space and here"—touching his chest—"in the equally vast reaches—inner space—everything is in order. Our task is to begin to understand that the Universal Mind is resident everywhere, and also, of necessity, within us. Our prayer is that the truth is made known, that it cannot fail to be revealed. This to you, Bernard, is mishmash. Right?"

"Right!" said Bernard.

But Bernard put both hands on his knees, elbows out, and seemed to be listening.

"I suggest, young fella, that the impersonal law of Love, operating in the universe, will take you where you want to go. In your present thinking you could set it into operation with a negative. Suppose we do. Dwell, day and night, on this: *I am ill. I am poor. I am wretched. I am a miserable sinner. There is no God. Blind chance in a glowering universe will soon strike me down.*

"Presently, sure enough, you'll be ill, poor, wretched and struck down. This is managed by many peoples with great ease. Whole nations do it. Now, on the other hand, reverse it, accept the flow of love that is available to each of us, take care with the environment you create for yourself, move up to a view from the tower and you'll find yourself in an improved climate making proper decisions. *The way we think is the way we act, and the way we act is what happens.* We have seen it work times without number.

"Now, then. Ideas are primary. Everything you see about you started as an idea. You want to be a realist—face this then: an idea became the Golden Gate Bridge. Ideas become freeways, concrete towers, chairs, loaves of bread, glass wine carafes resembling bunches of grapes; ideas become books, paintings, symphonies, governments. Wonders are wrought by affirmation when right ideas are held. We also have mountains of evidence that this is true.

"Will you consider that there is—behind symbolic words —a lot of *glue* in an idea of which we are all subconsciously aware each day of our lives?

"Consider, in this nation we have brought into friendly association European peoples—and Asians—who were once at each other's throats. Right now, with good will, we are engaged in solving a problem which has plagued mankind for centuries. We've blended diverse religions, social orders, creeds, colors, as well as it's ever been done. There is abundance here. Plant a seed in our soil and the earth goes mad with fruition. Why, we have such staggering abundance we become unpopular when we try to give some of it away. We've survived depressions, subversion, power grabs, crises and wars. What's holding it all together, Bernard, m'boy? A noble idea.

"Those four words IN GOD WE TRUST stand for the highest of concepts: a nation originating under moral law promising individual freedom and the greatest good to the greatest number. Such a concept, when universally acknowledged, becomes a cohesive force. When you've had a few demonstrations of your own, you'll be able to accept this as a possibility; at least you then would hesitate before attacking the pillars with a petition. Sorry, no deal."

Bernard was staring at him as if a new thought had broken through like a toggle bolt and was being locked inside. Later I heard him muttering, "An *idea* becomes a *cohesive force!*"

He was beginning to get it.

As the party was breaking up, Ernest's voice took on a gentle tone as he told me:

"When I saw that boy in the headlights with his thumb up, scared and arrogant and feisty and soft as butter, he reminded me of myself at nineteen. And in my day the problems were minor in comparison. Imagine being an adolescent in this decade with the old hellfire and damnation theories on one side, communism on the other, and all threatened by the bomb. They do pretty well, considering."

We went through the gate to his shiny new car. He had never subscribed to the convention that the minister should starve while the rest of the congregation grew more and more affluent in an affluent society. That particular car may have belonged to one of the ministers in the group and, thinking back now, I recall that Ernest often turned up in somebody else's car; he liked conversation and companionship while motoring and would often persuade a friend to drive him. It may have been due to his gift for detachment—he loved handsome cars but also could see himself low in the seat peering through the spokes of the wheel.

But he always looked tall enough to me; he was tall inside; tall on the platform; tall in his books, and stands taller among philosophers from year to year as time goes by.

It is just as well that we don't know when we are seeing a friend for the final time. We exchanged another anecdote or two and he drove away laughing. That is my last memory of him.

Time may prove that other philosophers with mightier reputations were lesser men.

Ernest Holmes was a public figure who didn't strive for fame. He offered to those who were ready to accept it a heart-lifting philosophy, gleaned from many sources but channeled through his own genius and presented in straightforward understandable terms. He would have been more widely known in his lifetime but he was wary of organization—recognized the need for some sort of structure but left the tasks to others. The people who were ready for his teaching would discover his books, he had always said; he had been content to lecture to a jam-packed theaterful every Sunday and go home. A philosopher needed time for reflection—and in his most productive years he had detached himself from the crowd at twelve o'clock on Sunday; a philosopher, not a minister—"See you next week!"

He was a man of many facets. What one observer finds true of him, another may dispute. In this account, as we present the evidentials, the case histories, the "answers to prayers," there'll be many another glimpse of Ernest Holmes etched in affection by men who believe they saw him clearly and held him in great esteem.

3

The Capital C Coincidences

There are techniques which any metaphysician constantly will employ when confronted with a problem; not mumbo-jumbo, not superstition, though to the skeptic our methods sometimes seem ridiculous. But the assumption that intelligence underlies all life is perfectly reasonable to those who have experienced the "Capital C Coincidence."

"When answers to prayer appear in an orderly and unspectacular way, your skeptical friends will tell you it's all a coincidence," Bernard Opley told me the next time I encountered him, which was in a garage in Ventura, California, long after our first meeting. "So I now call 'em Capital C Coincidences, and we're keeping a record, Dr. Hornaday. We've got twenty-four which *I* know are true. Not all big ones, of course. A small one just happened right here in this garage."

Bernard, whose name is fictional here, of course—we wouldn't want to embarrass a man whose working day is spent with skeptics—had grown up, married, graduated, and was now teaching in San Luis Obispo. He'd heard me preach in the Founder's Church, and remarked that he'd been glad to see all those comfortable seats filled with people. It reversed the propaganda that metropolitan churches were doomed because nobody would drive downtown on Sunday.

Our encounter itself had been a coincidence. I was driving north en route to a speaking engagement at Santa Barbara. My mind had been in the lofty upper reaches, thinking out my talk, when, a half mile south of Ventura, one end of the rear bumper fell off my brand-new car. For a few moments after that clank and rattle, nobody would have credited me with seeking the inner Light. I found myself grimly disapproving of Detroit and let myself become an outraged American motorist demanding of the heavens: Where are the craftsmen of yesteryear? Then, as usually happens at such times, my sense of humor gave me a nudge and my disgruntled self blushingly faded into the background as I thought, "Now, now, Bill, it's time to remember some of the things you say on Sundays."

I cautiously drove into town, rounded a corner, discovered an open door in a public garage, drove up the ramp and put on the brakes. There before me was a vaguely familiar outline; I puzzled it out and remembered. Bernard Opley was deep in an amiable chat with the garage foreman. He remembered, shook hands warmly and introduced me to the foreman who expressed profound regret on behalf of the car manufacturer. He did it well and I was soothed. Bernard invited me to the coffee bar at the back of the shop. He, too, had stopped for repairs, he said.

"Are you here through accident or treatment?" he asked.

I dropped my spoon in surprise.

"Oh, I'll never be religious," he explained quickly, "but this principle actually seems to work."

Ernest Holmes' books and pamphlets had sent him on a search, he told me, and then talked brightly of Plato, Plotinus, Emerson and Quimby.

"We're on the threshold of startling discoveries about the Power within," Bernard informed me. "You want to hear some of mine?"

The garage concoction of instant coffee and powdered cream had a character all its own. I needed it. Ernest seemed to be hovering behind us, chuckling. The impulsive rescue of a hitchhiker had made an enormous difference in this boy's thinking and therefore in his life. And this would have pleased Ernest. He wouldn't have asked for credit. But he would have been interested. He, too, would have pressed for details.

It turned out that as a result of his ride to Monterey, Bernard was now a happily married man.

"It's one of my Capital C Coincidences," he said, and promised to tell me all about it. He took out a notebook. "Lois and I are piling up these evidentials and keeping records, Dr. Hornaday. Remember one Sunday before Easter you preached on How to Pray Effectively? Well, we were there. We'd met for the first time the week before out in Pasadena—another Coincidence—and ever since then, when there's a problem, we try to approach it with what you called the Immanence of God."

"The phrase is borrowed. Ernest traced it back to Emerson, or even further," I told him. "To Plotinus, maybe. Plotinus had the concept of the Divine Mind in 252."

"Well, anyhow, when we change our thinking and reject

disaster, something good happens. Lois is keeping the record on file cards. We don't tell people because the skeptics laugh at you if you say you've had an answer to prayer. In fact, it seems to work best when we don't *call* it prayer."

"Why is that, do you suppose?"

"Well, everything's subjective, and *prayer* reminds me of our old hoe-down church and the hellfire and brimstone pouring like lava from the pulpit. It works when we think of it as enlarging our thinking or trusting the Power within. Then the solution comes like fog dissolving. I had an example of it right here in this garage."

The foreman interrupted. My bumper had now been securely bolted into place. There was no charge. I inwardly responded to the foreman's generosity and was grateful that no unkind words had been said about the nation's lost skill or Detroit's lack of integrity. There'd always be an occasional tired or careless workman, and now and again a lemon of a car. Once in a while a designer with a wild idea would test the taste of the nation. But by and large the motor industry produced chromium-plated marvels, the perfect car for the American state of mind and countryside.

"Sometimes," I confessed to Bernard, "I almost forget to practice what I preach." I stirred in the white vegetable powder. "Now, tell me about Lois."

"Well," he said, and now we had an eavesdropper, an oil-smudged redhead in blue coveralls who pretended not to be listening, as he sipped from a paper cup, "it goes back to the night Dr. Holmes talked about laws superseding other laws and the sinking bar of iron turning into the floating iron ship. That idea s-t-r-e-t-c-h-e-d something inside my skull. It erased the existentialism taught by a bug-eyed professor I'd had who'd convinced thirty-seven of us that everything added up to nothing. Because I'd believed him, things *were* adding up to nothing. So now I started on an affirmative kick—and affirmative things added up, too.

"I discovered there was a law in the universe that would let you have it any way you wanted: disaster or delight.

"That spring I watched a tree coming into leaf. Plants and trees seemed *conscious* of the spring. It was a miracle, and such miracles had been happening for a billion years. I decided to spend my week-ends and vacations studying the affirmative side—not to let myself be gulled, y'know, but *testing.*

"I began going to Religious Science churches. After the spring quarter, during the break, I visited a roommate down south here, which is about five hundred miles from Palo Alto, and I went to a beautiful new church, a very modern church with light pouring in the north window and white pews—it took the gloom out of Sunday for me.

"Well, they were serving coffee after church that morning and Lois Jessup was there with her grandmother, her mother's mother. Now, look; Lois and I have the same interests, but we'd never even seen each other before. She was from San Francisco, which is only a few minutes from Palo Alto, and she happened to be visiting in Los Angeles, which is fifteen minutes on the freeway from the church where we met. Her grandmother knew the minister. So there we were—a couple from northern California meeting for the first time five hundred miles from home! We both knew it was going to be permanent before we put down our coffee cups. We could talk to each other, y'know? Anyway, I've noticed as soon as you begin to study this philosophy you meet a lot of others who are also in it.

"Sometimes those in the movement turn out to be physicists or astronomers or lawyers, but because it isn't orthodox, many people either laugh or they're tolerant and faintly amused. You get used to condescension from characters who don't know anything about it and never tried it. It's best not to talk about it outside your own circle. You find you move into another dimension and your old pals either turn up inside the circle with you or painlessly fade away. And there you are sitting around a fireplace with an excited bunch of new friends cracking your brain trying to find out what it's all about."

"Was Lois attending college, too?"

"Yeah. But at Berkeley. She was a junior when we met. She lived with her Aunt Becky and I began to haunt their apartment. We were just pinned. We couldn't afford to get married until we graduated and were both teaching—Lois planned to teach in elementary school, the lower grades. Well, I was hanging around all hours and Aunt Becky said we ought to get formally engaged, and announce it so the neighbors would quit asking questions. One day I suddenly remembered Dr. Holmes' technique. Why shouldn't we not only get engaged but also married? *Now!* All we had to do was understand abundance. So we began to work this way—we decided to speak our Word and be confident and know that we could manage it as soon as we understood enough.

"Aunt Becky sent the announcement of our engagement to the San Francisco papers and it appeared in print with a picture of Lois. Well, the darndest coincidence happened. A few nights after the announcement appeared in print, a San Francisco lawyer named Mr. Cohen telephoned Lois and asked if she'd ever known a Will L. Jessup. Lois said her late grandfather was named Will L. Jessup. Mr. Cohen asked if Will Jessup ever lived in Canada and she said yes. Then he wanted to know how many direct descendents Will Jessup had? Well, she thought she was the only one. Her Aunt Becky, her mother's sister, had taken her in when she was little, when her folks were killed. Mr. Cohen asked a few more questions and hung up.

"We got pretty excited. We kinda *bore down* on our technique. Lois racked her memory trying to recall things about her grandfather. He'd been a Canadian, all right, and used to explore for oil, only he ended up as an American citizen, and broke. He died in Glendora, California, with just about enough to bury him. But we began to think maybe an old oil well had suddenly spurted; we could just see one of those pumps going *a-dollar, a-dollar, a-dollar,* you know the way they do.

"We were so sure we'd rubbed the lamp and got the genie out building us a castle that when *I* got a hundred dollars for a thing I sent to the *Reader's Digest,* we took Aunt Becky with us for a witness one winter day and got married. Aunt Becky said we could stay with her until we built our own place. We had a nice apartment there to come back to. Lois wanted a honeymoon at Twentynine Palms—oh, well, that's another story.

"Anyhow, Mr. Cohen called a couple more times. It sure looked good for a while. Mr. Cohen said the way it all started was, he'd been up in Canada visiting a friend, a newspaper editor in Victoria, British Columbia. Mr. Cohen always read the legal ads, of course, and one day he'd noticed a law firm in Vancouver advertising for any living relatives of Will L. Jessup. A few days later back in San Francisco when he saw our announcement, the name rang a bell so he sent to Canada for the back issue of *The Vic-*

toria Times. Then he phoned Lois. Then he wrote the law firm in Vancouver. He told us we were going to hear from them presently, and sure enough we did.

"They wrote that a man named Thomas R. Rowe—a name Lois had never heard of—had been Will Jessup's boyhood friend. One early spring day Thomas R. Rowe went through some rubber ice on Ring Lake and would have drowned except that Will L. Jessup pulled him out. Rowe never forgot. He didn't have a lot of money when he died but he left a thousand dollars to Will L. Jessup, who was already gone, so it came to his heirs.

"Well, it wasn't an oil well, but it was better than a poke in the eye with a sharp-pointed stick. However, the money was delayed. Then they wrote and said it looked like they'd found Will L. Jessup's second cousin in Rochester, New York. And so forth. Finally, after the taxes were paid and all that, Lois got a check for five hundred and eighty-two dollars and ninety-seven cents.

"It was all just a coincidence, of course. But then we got to thinking: we were married. We were happy.

"Aunt Becky had fixed up her old sewing room and the back bedroom into an apartment for us, and you couldn't ask for anything finer. We were studying together and doing better because we were both getting enough sleep. Aunt Becky is a gourmet cook, with a lot of nice silverware and china, and the meals were superb. Aunt Becky was grateful for our companionship, and we had privacy and comfort and elegant dinners and no rent to pay—how could we have had more abundance if there'd been oil wells? If we needed cash, we had the five hundred and eighty. Oh, yes. We tried to pay Mr. Cohen for his trouble but he said no, just invite him to the wedding. So we had to tell him we'd already been married. He invited us to dine with him in San Francisco.

"He was a jolly little man and in the restaurant—one we could never have afforded—the headwaiter treated him like he was Mr. San Francisco in person. He was a wonderful man, and we made a new friend—and guess what? His late wife had been a student of Ernest Holmes'! We found that out just as we were saying good night.

"It's like what I said about your old pals, you know? You start *thinking* this way, one thing leads to another, and you find yourself dining with a famous lawyer in a famous restaurant, and he's your new friend and interested in the same—"

A loud-speaker blasted:

"Jim Foster wanted at the service desk. Jim Foster!"

Our eavesdropper started convulsively; we had both forgotten him.

"Look," Jim Foster said hastily, "I was gonna ask you—my wife's mother got over arthritis reading a book, that's what *she* says, but I never believed it. Know what she did? Imagined herself running barefoot along the beach the way she used to as a girl. But, also, she changed her diet. And pretty soon she was well. It was the diet that did it. That's what *I* say."

"It was a Coincidence," Bernard said. "But maybe her deep self knew what she needed and as soon as she worked positively, and rejected negative ideas of resentment and worry, a miracle happened. She saw herself well again! I can tell you this—my deep self knows where to go for car repairs—and I can prove it."

The amplifiers were chanting impatiently. Jim Foster had to go; he left reluctantly and Bernard went on:

"Dr. Hornaday, you remember the night we talked about Aladdin's lamp? Well, Lois and I discovered it's not that easy—it isn't rubbing the lamp and suddenly there's a genie building you a castle. It isn't spectacular; it isn't magic. But when that thousand-dollar Coincidence happened, we said we'd keep on working for more of these Coincidences and take a chance. You got time to hear about our honeymoon?"

"I wouldn't miss it," I assured him. Already I was mulling over an idea for next Sunday's sermon; and this, thanks to almost losing a bumper. Nothing but good is going on when we have the courage to accept it as the basic idea.

"Well, sir"—Bernard hooked his heels on the high stool and his wry half-grin reminded me of the boy he had been —"Lois wanted to honeymoon at an old adobe inn in Twentynine Palms. It had been a dream of hers for years. Each cottage at the inn has a fireplace and a patio; very cozy. So I made reservations, and we started out. I misjudged the distance.

"After the wedding we took Aunt Becky home and then started south on 101. We got into the desert beyond Paso Robles long after dark and began to run into No Vacancy signs. It grew windy and cold. There were eerie joshua trees and a vast skyful of stars and a few lights in desert shacks, miles apart, and no other traffic—it was a back road. About midnight we found a vacant tourist cabin with linoleum on the floor and oilcloth on the table. It was clean enough and Lois was willing to stay. She was afraid I might fall asleep at the wheel. But I'm a snob, Dr. Hornaday. I didn't want to start married life in a four-dollar tourist cabin, and I said we'd take turns and drive all night and get to Twentynine Palms in the morning and sleep then.

It was a crazy idea; after all the excitement we were exhausted. Lois hadn't had a real night's sleep for a week. Girls have a lot to do when they get married, even if it's informal.

"Well, we drove on. She dozed for a while and then she suddenly woke up and said: 'Bernard—what's wrong with us! Let's try for a Coincidence.' I said, 'Why, sure.'

"So I treated this way, I said: 'I affirm my acceptance of a safe journey and proper accommodations for a honeymoon couple. The Power within will tell me how to manage this. Two travelers in a well-ordered universe will have a successful journey.'

"We were still doing this, and feeling pretty confident, too, when there was a flash way to the north. We decided it had been an airplane crash. Pretty soon a searchlight began slashing the sky. We figured it was maybe ten miles away to the northwest. Then we came to an airport sign—nine miles. This was in the wrong direction but it looked like a distress signal so I swung the car to the right and we headed across the desert on a brand-new six-lane road.

"I suppose you're ahead of me? The light turned out to be an advertisement for a brand-new motel on opening night with one double room left, free champagne and an orchid corsage for the ladies. I signed Mr. and Mrs. Bernard Opley for the first time and we were both kinda shaking, for *every* reason. It was as if we really had a genie!"

"Pure coincidence, of course?" I asked, believing it to be much more.

"*Is* it?"

"What do *you* think?"

"I don't know, sir. I'm still a student. You want to hear how I happened to be in this garage right this minute?"

"I do if I don't have to drink any more coffee." He grinned, went over to the coke machine and came back with two bottles. I sipped gratefully.

"This is a quickie," he said, and I thought he looked very earnest, as if he wanted to convince me.

"I've been down in Los Angeles for a teacher's meeting and there was something wrong with my car, a queer grinding noise that came and went; it was alarming. I met up with three not-too-honest mechanics: two on the way down, and one while I was there. Each time it cost me about twelve dollars. I found this out: when you admit you don't know anything about motors, they charge you twelve dollars: eleven seventy-five or twelve thirty-six. They charge you for being naive. I'll never do it again.

"Anyhow, when I'd traveled about fourteen miles this morning the grinding started again so I wheeled into a gas station. The man said it was the universal and although it was Saturday he'd stay and work overtime and take it apart. Then I remembered that I hadn't even tried the philosophy; I'd had too many other things on my mind. I said no, thanks, and started grinding north. But then I went to *work* for a Coincidence. I treated this way:

"Reduce this car to atoms and the atoms to energy and the energy to thought on the positive side," I said, "and this car becomes *an idea of transportation.* It will last long enough to get me to an honest mechanic. I now affirm that I will find an honest mechanic in ample time. I will trust my own consciousness, the Power within; I will instinctively know which garage to turn into.

"So I drove along into Ventura. There were many open garages, and it was getting toward noon, when they close, but nothing happened inside me—no hunch. So I just kept going. I felt kind of serene, can't explain it, but I felt prescient, you know? I *knew* something good was going to happen. I turned a corner on Main Street, here was this wide-open garage door, so I drove in here. That foreman's a nice guy, a Dane. He took my car around the block. Then he started to grin. We drove back here, he crawled underneath on that little wheeled cart, tightened something with a wrench and came rolling back out in about forty seconds. My muffler had been riding against the gear housing. It was now all fixed.

"I tried to pay him, but he said he'd enjoyed talking to me and to drop in next time I came through. So! It's a little bit of a thing, Dr. Hornaday. It's just a coincidence. But we've got twenty-four of 'em in our file, including the thousand dollars which became five hundred and eighty-two from out of the wild blue Canadian sky."

As we got up to go, I said:

"Ernest used to say—'Never be astonished when prayer is answered; be surprised when it isn't—and find out where *you* went wrong.' "

"I might buy that."

We exchanged addresses and I drove on north thinking about the first time I'd heard an Ernest Holmes lecture at the Institute, and my awakening in China which had so conditioned me to another way of thinking that I could listen for an hour on Sunday to a man who at first had sounded almost sacrilegious.

That first lecture was a provocative experience for a onetime orthodox missionary-to-be who had gone to China full of honest ardor to save the heathen. My family had already boasted three generations of ministers, and this had marked me. But the changes in the intellectual climate in the twentieth century which upset the religious belief of so many young people were already sweeping through the world. I'd got a whiff of a fresh breeze somewhere. But even so I was rigid for quite a while.

My own training had been lifelong. My father had been a minister and I loved and admired him. He had been a circuit rider. My grandfather was an evangelist. I'd grown up on tales of Grandpa's contest with the devil in Nebraska and thereabouts. In my family we spoke glibly of "sin and damnation" and used many of the phrases which were even then driving the Bernard Opleys from the churches.

A Science of Mind student could reinterpret the clichés of such orthodoxy and demonstrate that we had common ground. "Being saved for Jesus" might mean dedication to the search for the Christ Consciousness. "Let this mind be in you, which was also in Christ Jesus" * was a sweeping concept given to the world in a letter from Paul to the Philippians and no doubt led to much of the early interpretive work of the metaphysicians.

The world which had existed for billions of years had not been without the Christ Spirit. The Christ Consciousness has always been here and always will be. The notion that the earlier centuries had been without help from heaven had been an enormous stumbling block in my youth. It seemed so unfair. I couldn't bear to think about it; and it was probably nudging me subconsciously when, in my ardor, I sailed to China with a halfhearted plan to become a missionary.

In China my language teacher despaired of me from the start. The nasal singsong refused to issue from my vocal cords and nostrils. My Chinese characters looked like

* Philippians 2:5.

Rorschach inkblots. There was within me an unrecognized awareness which was subtly sabotaging my efforts. That is a paradox, of course, an "unrecognized awareness," but as we learn more about the vast undercurrents which lead us toward an awakening to the knowledge which we already possess—an opening of our minds to the universal knowledge which is ours, and always has been—we begin to understand why a young man who honestly thinks he wants to become a missionary can, at the same time, unknowingly engage in sabotaging the enterprise.

Put it this way: my father's son, my grandfather's grandson, the Hornaday whom the neighbors said would grow up to be "a preacher, too, praise be!" was out in the world performing exactly as the family and the neighborhood expected. He had in no way endangered anybody's status, including his own. But the individual soul-aware Hornaday, the maturing child of his century, touched by the winds of change, nudged by a growing recognition of discoveries in the fields of science which ran counter to an old concept, was already further on the road to heresy than he suspected.

This was the sort of soul struggle a Passionist Monk once suffered on a balcony in Switzerland, thoughtfully considering the speed of light as he watched the winter stars in an immeasurable universe. Overnight his vocation was gone. A universe in evolution! In Spiritual evolution? And had he accepted a naive concept of Time? It called for rethinking his position. Just so. A religion to be accepted by an honest young man in mid-twentieth century must square with the wisdom of his day; this was the stirring going on under the surface. It remained only for him to discover that the heathen he had come to save knew more about religion than he did, and it was as though a crust had broken in his mind. Icy breezes blew.

And what the heathen taught the missionary-to-be is worth recording.

4

Lesson from a Buddhist

This is how it happened.

At this distance he can be viewed with detachment: a tall young man, immature and narrow in his religious thinking, looking about him in distress at the poor heathen shuffling into temples to pray to a God that never was! Obviously, they were all doomed—unless some could be saved by an ardent Christian from Monterey Park, California, U.S.A.

He would begin by learning the Chinese language. Then he could convey the good news in the heathen's own tongue, and in a hurry!

This was where the self-sabotage came in; my instructor despaired of teaching me in the orthodox fashion. It was arranged for me to live for a short time with a Chinese family in the hope that through daily association I'd pick up what could not be gleaned from textbook and classroom.

I went forth with my suitcase to a middle-class Chinese home.

The family greeted me with exquisite courtesy; nobody spoke a word of English, but the attitude of my host, his wife, and his sons was eloquent enough. They were kind, considerate, sensitive for others as well as for themselves, generous, loving, gay. Like Christians?

It gradually dawned on me that their religion, whatever it might be, was practiced twenty-four hours a day. The idols—and they were everywhere—were symbols of the Power in which they believed.

There was, for instance, a God of Sleep. It was a wooden image, a serene, chubby face with the eyes closed in slumber.

Learning from his sons one morning that I had tossed the night away, my host told me as I came groggily to breakfast that, come evening, the God of Sleep would arrange for me to have a good night's rest. There would be a small ceremony first.

After dinner—and I was doing pretty well with the chopsticks by this time, and was warmed by praise—my host brought the God of Sleep to the table and lifted off the top of his head.

"You are now assured of sweet repose," he pronounced, "but may I ask—what would you like to dream about?"

"Home," I said promptly, and recognized the ache I'd been carrying in my heart.

He masked an understanding smile as he wrote on a slip of paper and placed it in the idol.

"It shall be," he said, and put the lid back on.

Render unto Caesar the things that are Caesar's; when in Rome do as the Romans do; rationalize: this is a heathen worship and a heathen idol, but these people are well-intentioned. I asked myself, what harm can it do?

I went to bed, fell asleep as my head hit the pillow and dreamed happily of home.

Of course I had succumbed to suggestion. I was tired, anyway; it was a coincidence.

But a new concept crept into a closed and narrow young mind.

Before long I began asking questions. Once when trying to understand the meaning of a religious ritual, my host, who was a Buddhist, asked how Christianity was practiced. This was a glorious chance. I talked with ardor and quoted at length the Commandments of Jesus and my church's dogma.

He was gravely thoughtful.

"Do you really love everybody?" he asked, looking directly into my eyes. "Do you really bless them that persecute you?"

"I try," I said stoutly, and succumbed to a fit of coughing.

He had been concerned that morning because I had the symptoms of a cold.

"You are not angry at anyone?" he asked. "Sometimes emotional stress causes a cold. Is it not true?"

That, too, was a new idea—new to me, but four thousand years old to the Chinese.

Gently, he suggested that I join him in a Buddhist service. Honestly believing that the wrath of God would be upon me, I declined.

He was philosophical. "Yet, it is our duty to take note of how we feel within ourselves about ourselves and about others," he told me gently. "When this has been done properly, we find ourselves in perfect balance."

I assured him that I felt all right, really I did.

"Yet you are prejudiced." His tone was mild. "You don't understand our belief and are not willing to let me explain."

There was justice in this.

"Well, go ahead," I capitulated. "Tell me about it."

"On the contrary," he smiled, "I will let you tell yourself."

After we were seated on the floor near a shrine, he brought out two beautifully carved, hand-sized blocks of ivory. The backs of the blocks were smooth; the inside, exquisitely carved, presented a landscape scene with human figures, tiny bridges, shrubbery; the insides of the blocks complemented each other and when brought together fitted perfectly.

He placed them on the floor before me.

"The first requirement is to be honest with oneself," he said. "If you are prejudiced toward anyone, move them a few inches apart."

Prejudiced? After a moment of soul searching I managed to meet his eye. He was too courteous to permit himself to smile, but there was a sense of suppressed amusement as I moved the blocks a few inches apart. He had said a *few*, not a yard. I took him at his word.

"If you are afraid of any person, place, or thing, again you must move them apart," he said.

Afraid? There was menace everywhere in that strange land. Of course I was afraid.

I moved the blocks again. They were now a foot apart.

"If you feel guilty over something you have done in the past—move them again."

In the world I'd lived in, the path was straight and narrow, and almost everything enjoyable was wrong. I was hagridden with guilt. I settled on another several inches.

"If you are uncertain about your relationship with a Power greater than yourself, move them once again."

I stretched and put them where I felt they should go.

"This is good," said my host. "You are honest. Now, take all the thoughts that you have used to separate the ivories and *reverse them*—for prejudice can be erased with love and understanding; fear disappears as one grows in strength and wisdom; guilt should not accompany a young man who means to do his best for all other men; and the recognition of a Power within greater than the small self is like a flower opening to the sun, the true beginning of the love of God. There. This is your religious service.

"When you have forgiven yourself and others, when you have recognized that all life is God, that that life is within you, then you can bring the blocks together in wholeness; you will feel better, and life henceforth will be more meaningful."

It was an hour that would be with me from then on; it was the first time I had been called upon to do for myself the things I'd prayed that God would do for me. I settled down to it with furrowed brow.

It was a struggle to bring the blocks together: the heathen had turned the would-be missionary inside out and made a Christian of him—or, at any rate, enlarged his view, revealing the universality of the Power within, preparing him, though he was slow to acknowledge this, for his encounter with a remarkable philosopher who was to become his friend and mentor.

From then on, in bounding good health, I actually began to see China and to know the Chinese people and to love them. I had been softened up.

The day I reluctantly left that Chinese family my host spoke English for the first time—and spoke it perfectly. He confessed that he was a graduate of a university in the United States where he had majored in agriculture.

"You learned faster because you couldn't lean on me," he explained, smiling. "We have great resources within ourselves when we are forced to use them."

We shook hands warmly all around and I left them with their religion intact and went back to America enlightened.

So there it was. The missionary-to-be had had a shock in a Chinese home. He soon enlarged his view—somewhat—broadened his reading—somewhat. But my carefully structured belief was gone. I still believed in God, yes; but no longer could my faith sustain the creaking mechanism which had propped God up for a weekly presentation. I had been an easy victim for a gentle Oriental whose Buddhist views seemed more Christian than my own.

A swift review of the years that followed revealed a story like that of many another man who is unsure of what he wants from life. I started my own business, and a profitable one, joined the commuters, married, bought a hilltop house in Altadena, settled down to succeed, play golf, drive a new car, raise a family, buy an annuity, retire and await the end. Or so it began to seem.

Unless a man's heart is in it, business can become sound and fury signifying nothing.

I was doing well but, they tell me now, I sighed a lot. And stood at the window gazing at the mountains. Went for long walks. Was abstracted . . . um? What did you say?

Then a member of my family announced at dinner one Sunday that she had attended a church-in-a-theater where a man named Ernest Holmes presented a religious philosophy as if he knew—for sure—what he was talking about.

Her instinct was sound. Ernest Holmes had worked out a philosophy that satisfied his questioning mind and could be illustrated on a blackboard and conveyed in eloquent lectures to those willing to hear.

And, it could be proved.

My first encounter with him was at a Sunday morning lecture. We arrived early in order to get a seat. As a man who had seen his share of empty pews I was startled to find that people were being turned away at the door long before the service began.

Dr. Ernest Holmes was a short man who walked tall. He had no reverence for ecclesiasticism or outmoded theology. He said the Power within was available to all men, saint or sinner, without intercession by priest or pastor, without mediator. When his words began to reach me, I was shocked. But all around me people were taking notes. It was like a college lecture.

Outside we ran into a university professor whom we knew and respected. He said: "Provocative, isn't he?"

That was a mild word: provocative.

But some of the phrases came back to me during the week. He had said:

"Man is a manifestation of Spirit and for Spirit to desire evil for him would be for It to desire evil for Itself. All apparent evil is the result of ignorance and will disappear to the degree that it is no longer thought about or indulged in."

My route to the office took me along streets where I passed many a hovel. Were tenements a state of mind, I wondered? Were they a part of what Holmes had meant?

It was a fresh concept for the onetime soul-saver. Yet,

what if the dreary drunk I had glimpsed sitting with his blinding hangover on a front step—what if he had spent last evening at a lecture? Suppose in his search for understanding of the glorious universe all about him he had brought home a challenging thought—new and practical. Suppose, this morning, he had awakened with a new hope! Suppose out of this had come a decision. Yes—let's follow this: he would make a decision. That decision would carry him into the city. He would hopefully look for work.

The *quality* of his awareness and the degree of his training would put him with like-minded people. His affirmation would result in his being hired. His work would place him on a level where he was capable of function. As he learned more about his job, wisdom would come—*ignorance would no longer be indulged in,* Ernest Holmes' phrase. And as he improved his function and enlarged his concepts, he would naturally change his environment—and eventually, when he glanced back, that tenement would have been only a state of mind!

Provocative.

On another Sunday, after driving into town alone, I slipped into a side seat in the theater a few minutes after the lecture had begun. My notes are still here in a ten cent notebook:

> Many who had lost faith in God have, in this new manner of thinking, found what their souls had sought. The emphasis is insistently on God, ever present, ever available; and man's ability to make himself receptive to the inflow of the Divine Spirit. In essence this is the primal message of enlightened prophets of all ages, and this is the message of Religious Science.

Monday morning, driving to work, the phrase *receptive to the inflow of Divine Spirit* began to run in my mind like a singing commercial. Had I been receptive to the inflow of the Divine Spirit, and was I now? *Receptive.* What did that mean, exactly? That night we sought the dictionary for the exact meaning—the first of many times when the dictionary illuminated a half-understood metaphysical idea.

Receptive: Able or inclined to take in, absorb, hold, or contain.

All right then. I was, it seems, *inclined.* I was also *able*—to take in. How about *absorb?* How could I absorb this teaching—so that I would forever experience the inflow of the Divine Spirit? Well, *absorb,* in this sense, then, meant *study.* If I studied, I would understand it—if there were something here to be understood—and in that event I would hold or contain it.

The next Sunday found me down in front, early, with a larger notebook. I was closer to the bright intelligent eye and the inner glow. This was one of his hard-hitting days.

> Unless there were a *method* for spiritual mind practice, then such practice would not be scientific. Unless there were a definite technique its use could not be taught. Some people are fortunate enough to possess absolute conviction and faith through intuition. But all do not have this. And if we waited for Divine Power to be released only to those who possess such faith there would be little hope for the rest of us.

These words in somewhat altered form appeared in one of his books. There is nothing in that paragraph now to convey its impact on me that morning. Studied now, the expression is clear enough but not especially distinguished, and what is said now strikes me as obvious. But the words *method* and *technique* were tangibles appearing in a fog bank. My religion had been challenged in a Chinese home. Belief and faith had taken on an awakened overtone, but there were questions still to be answered.

Ernest continued:

> In metaphysical practice we arrive at this conviction through a process of thinking. The process itself is not the conviction, it is the road that leads to it. The student must be willing to subject his mind to conscious self-training until there comes into his thinking a clear realization of truth, which the *intuition feels* and the intellect must, or may, proclaim.

My note ends: *How about that!*

I find there three lines under intellect and an exclamation mark. Intellect, I had come to think, had to be left at the door of my old church like Chinese slippers; only misty emotion could be taken inside.

There is firm underlining beneath the words *intuition feels.* Here was something that struck me as being profound —a willingness to test the philosophy against what *intuition feels.* There *is* a still small voice functioning within us. There *is* a deep awareness which will make itself known when we get ourselves out of the way—when we have the courage to move aside. Dr. Holmes was saying "to test the philosophy—with the intuition *and* the intellect."

The need now was to find a God my intellect and intuition could accept without reservation. I needed to worship. I needed the misty moral emotionalism, too, perhaps. But my soul-searching had torn away layers of false beliefs. It was time to begin at bedrock.

Into my excitement came Holmes' words:

"The spiritual practioner does not make a demonstration by saying peace when there is no peace. He makes a demonstration only when confusion is converted into peace. The authority of his words rests finally on what those words accomplish. The results prove the theory."

And that was what everything in me was longing to hear. *The results would prove the theory.*

I would enroll at the Institute and study this new religion. If there were techniques, I would learn them. If they proved out, I would accept them.

I would be "receptive to the inflow of Divine Spirit" but I wouldn't be led into mistaking a physical sense of well-being for the Spirit of God.

Now, hold on! Wouldn't that *be* the Spirit of God?

There always would be a sense of physical well-being if one were truly receptive to the inflow of the Divine Spirit. Wasn't that true? There were healthy, cheerful-looking people at those services.

One Sunday I'd heard a woman say as we were leaving:

"I haven't had a cold in six years—not since the first Sunday I began to get *the idea.*"

"I wouldn't be caught dead with a cold," the other woman said.

Snatches of lobby conversation amused me. It was talk unlike any I'd ever heard. Each seemed to be on a different level of understanding, but all were working to be "receptive to the inflow of Divine Spirit." Yet how easy to be self-deceived, I thought. And how much of all this was self-hypnosis? In what Dr. Holmes called "subjecting the mind to conscious self-training," wasn't there a degree of self-hypnosis?

When we were introduced after the service, it was obvious that someone had already spoken to Dr. Holmes about me.

"Come and talk to me when you've time, Bill," Holmes said. "They tell me you're a preacher." The word was said with an odd inflection; the half-taunting overtone belied the friendliness in his eyes.

"My training included preaching," I responded stiffly. "I'm not preaching now."

"Are you getting anything out of these lectures?"

"I find them provocative," I quoted.

"That's good. I do, too. There's a lot I say that I don't understand myself. It was pretty clear to me this morning, but sometimes it's almost too complex for anybody like me to understand."

He was kidding. Or was he?

Thereafter, we had exchanges nearly every Sunday. He would ask me to step aside and chat awhile. One day he asked me to have lunch with him. He did himself very well indeed; no modern philosopher should be narrowly aware of the right side of the menu, he said. He taught abundance on Sunday and believed his own life should manifest abundance. The earth was fruitful. Rivers and seas overflowed with fishes. Plant a seed in well-fertilized soil, water it—and you had to jump aside to avoid being speared by the grain. All the world's threadbare preachers and their threadbare offspring wearing the banker's kid's hand-me-downs had the wrong idea. Life was joyous, the earth abounded, all was superlatively well.

"I hear you come from a family of ministers; that right, Bill?"

"Three generations or so," I answered, and changed the subject. "Will you tell me sometime how you arrived at your philosophy, Dr. Holmes?"

"I'll tell you right now in three words," he said. "I stole it."

It was a shock and he was pleased.

"You can't steal the truth, though," he amended. "If the central idea of my philosophy is true, then it's yours. And his." He pointed to the next table. "And hers. And mine. Truth existed before any of us came on the scene. One's manner of expression can be trademarked, but what we are teaching at the Institute has been gleaned from the wisdom of the ages, east and west, and if it's true, it belongs to anybody who can understand it."

In the elevator I was aware of a measuring glance.

"Do you like your present job, Bill?"

"Y-yes," I said, and added heartily, "Yes, I do. I manage my own business."

"What is it?"

"Educational toys."

"Why did you hesitate just now?"

"Well," I tried to laugh, "I'm recovering. Last week a whole planeload of Ant Villages had to be scrapped. Five thousand frames. The ants died enroute to New York."

"Died!" His sympathy was with the ants. "Five thousand!"

"Five thousand villages—glass-and-frame villages—about half a million ants. We had to pay freight both ways. It was quite a loss."

"Ant Villages? How did you get into that?"

While an undergraduate at Whittier College, I had constructed a glass-and-frame Ant Village to illustrate a paper I'd written for my science course. Instantly, clamoring small boys in the neighborhood stormed my weekend workshop with requests for villages of their own. I dreamed up sermons while constructing Ant Villages in my spare time.

I was preaching in Monterey Park every Sunday as a substitute for my father—a very young man preaching very impassioned sermons. My dad, trying to round out fifty years in the ministry, in spite of ill health, had held onto his parish with only a few months remaining before his retirement.

Before long I found myself in business with more orders than I could handle. Bullock's, Marshall Field's, Macy's, Neiman-Marcus, stores everywhere hurled orders at me. But after Dad retired, I closed up shop and then, starry-eyed with sense of mission, went off to save the Chinese—only to discover Christlike gentlefolk in a Buddhist home.

On the way back from China I stood in the bow of the ship asking myself: "What do I believe? Shall I continue my Search for Truth, or go back to business?"

The answer came quickly. During my absence the "Ant Village" craze had really taken hold—undoubtedly due to the use of one of my original villages in a Van Johnson–June Allyson picture, "The Bride Goes Wild." The stores welcomed me. They had had thousands of requests for Ant Villages. They'd been unable to supply the demand. In no time at all it was big business. Molds for a new model, Ant Castles, were purchased at the cost of thousands of dollars and before long the newspapers were wryly calling me "The Ant King."

"I supplied the ants for Cecil B. DeMille's 'Samson and Delilah.' " I told Ernest modestly.

He didn't seem impressed.

"You like living in Altadena?"

"Very much. Yes. The whole family is happy."

"A hilltop house, and all that?"

"Quite a comfortable house, yes. It's a peaceful suburb."

"Uh-huh. Tell me, what caused the trouble in the five thousand villages?"

"A new substance in the paint used on the frames poisoned the ants."

"The poison dissipated in time, I suppose?"

"Well, no. We thought it had. But in the end we were forced to junk all the frames and start over."

"Costly."

"Put it down as the hazards of business." Again I tried to laugh. "They let you take it off your income tax."

We walked on toward the parking lot. Ernest that day was squared off by a brown-checked sports jacket and dark green pleated slacks which put his five feet three inches at sea level.

"Bill," he said, adjusting the cushion in his car, "I think you ought to know that I've been *treating* because I need a preacher. My Sunday service has been standing room only for so long I had to start off one of our teachers in another theater. He's had a better offer—in a church—and he's leaving. I'll talk to the trustees about you. A *preacher* teaching Science of Mind could fill that theater. It's the Belmont, you know."

"How many seats?"

"Sixteen hundred."

"How large is the attendance?"

"It's not anywhere near what it should be," he admitted. "The man who is leaving is very able, one of our best, but he isn't a *preacher,* and that's what they seem to want. I'm finally convinced you can't educate these people away from preaching. They even want to sing hymns." He glanced around, as if to see if anyone were listening. "They're trying to get me to put on a robe, too. To start up again the same old rigmarole I worked so hard to get rid of, and maybe I'm weakening. Maybe if it makes them feel better, they should have it. Not much of it, not all that *machinery*, but some. The audience is supposed to *think* at my lectures, and some do, but many cannot settle down until they've heard a solo and sung a hymn."

He broke off to tell me about a young singer with an evangelist troupe who recently had assured the religious press that he'd been converted to Christianity while listening to a tape-recorded playback of his own rendition of an ancient hymn.

"A sense of humor would be an unsupportable handicap to many preachers," Ernest said. "But something ought to be established at the Belmont the way people want it, within reason. Personally, I don't like any falderal. I just want to teach, and that's it."

He probed at me with his bright blue eyes. "Since I've been treating on this need for a preacher-teacher, it's only fair to tell you that the first time I saw you something in me said: This could be the man."

I felt a slight chill.

"I have only a vague idea of your philosophy—"

"You're attending classes in the evening."

"Yes, I am. And getting a lot out of it. But my business is satisfying—"

"Is it? Who catches the ants?"

"I have ant catchers on the Mojave Desert," I answered stiffly. You can't say "ant catchers" and make it sound like cowboys at the round-up.

"Ant catchers on the Mojave," he nodded, and had the kindness not to smile. "Well." He suddenly shook hands with me. "If you aren't the one for the Belmont, we'll soon know. But I've put the Word in action, so here we are."

That was the substance of the conversation, and a few months later I closed the business, sold the house, moved my family nearer town and into smaller quarters.

But I kept the molds for the Ant Castles and enough odds and ends to start up again if necessary. We rented a nearby garage and stored them, neatly catalogued and ready to resume business. At the same time there was no lack of faith in this; I was a businessman, and the molds were worth money.

Yet I'd begun to feel that I was home again. In one course at the Institute, a slim book by Ernest Holmes, *Your Invisible Power,* became an open door to spiritual understanding. Intelligence and intuition agreed: I would be receptive to the new teaching—and the results would prove the theory. The ministry was in my blood and I would settle into something worth the time and effort.

On the Saturday before my first appearance at the Belmont, I dropped in at the Institute to arrange for a soloist and flowers on the platform.

Ernest Holmes snapped a finger in self-rebuke when he saw me. Then he led me into his office and closed the door.

"Didn't get around to talking to the trustees until just yesterday," he admitted sheepishly. "They're not too enthusiastic about the Belmont, Bill."

I felt around for a seat.

"Naturally," he said, going behind his big desk to the swivel chair, "I told them I'll not be a party to closing anything down. This work has to *progress.* But I wanted to warn you—we're on our own there. Some of the trustees feel that you're too new to the work, and a minister better known to the metaphysical movement should be engaged. They question your ability to raise the necessary money to pay rent, salaries, and so forth. But that can't make any difference."

"No difference!" I hadn't discussed this with him because it was too dismal. "There was only a small congregation in the Belmont last Sunday when I went there to observe the service."

"Did it rain?"

"No."

"The point is, Bill, we understand the law of abundance. You're going to have a golden chance to prove out the Principle."

Irritation crept into my voice.

"I don't mind saying, sir, I'm very uneasy about this."

My wife was even then returning to the senders, with an apologetic note, orders for the Ant Villages. We hadn't been able to find anybody with enough knowledge of ants *and* enough money *and* the enterprise to take over.

"Uneasy, are you?"

"Frankly, yes. Here we are, just getting your overflow and the ones who don't want to drive that far, because you're six miles away."

Ernest preached in Beverly Hills in a charming theater just off Wilshire. The Belmont was on Vermont Avenue in Los Angeles. His overflow had to make a sleeper jump. Belatedly it all began to seem very impractical.

"Bill?"

"Sir?"

"Do you think you can bear the consequences of the way you're thinking?"

The remark entered my head somewhere between my eyes. I suspect my ears picked it up after it had been rattling around inside for a moment. *Could I bear the consequences of the way I was thinking?* Well, the way I was thinking had been the manner of thought of the ardent young man in Monterey Park—the dedicated substitute minister who was able to entice neighborhood youngsters into Sunday school by making them Ant Villages in his spare time. The consequences of that kind of thinking had sent him to China and back, into Altadena and out of it, into business and out of it.

"No, I can't," I confessed. "I'll reverse it."

"Then let's treat for the answer," he said. "There are no obstructions in Bill's pathway; no hindrance to his endeavors at the Belmont. Let our word be the Law of elimination to all thought of hindrance. We behold the Belmont service as a perfect action of Truth and see that it is even now done, complete and perfect. And so it is."

Then Ernest added, "That's good. It's done, Bill. Now, go and prove the Principle. Dr. Reginald Armor will help you."

But in proving the principle there was no desire to take the spiritual path to a Rolls-Royce or to positively think my way into a world cruise and a house at Newport. Now that I had graduated from the Institute, it was to be hoped that Science of Mind would lead to a spiritual understanding of the universe, of myself and my mission—if I had one. It was the realm of the Spirit and its outward expression that I was seeking.

But the world around me was real enough, and in seeking the realm of the Spirit there was an immediate practical need to prove that my understanding of the teaching could produce six thousand dollars to keep the Belmont open—and dispel any doubts in the minds of the trustees.

I started for the theater that Sunday morning very much aware of the late Rev. W. H. D. Hornaday, Sr., the Methodist circuit rider. There was a cheerful greeting at the door. Then my footsteps echoed across the empty stage. Gladioli bristled in tall vases. I waited in the wings until eleven and then went out to the high-backed chair and saw the empty seats stretching away to the galleries. One hundred and twelve from sixteen hundred. We had one thousand four hundred and eighty-eight empty seats.

Prove the Principle, Ernest had said.

Room to expand, I told myself, which was the affirmative way to approach it.

5

Sagebrush Sam Speaks the Word

Always when we pray we must believe.
—ERNEST HOLMES

Easier said than done. Indeed, so easily said that the significance of the words can be lost in a glib repetition. What is meant by "belief?" The Bernard Opleys long ago rejected the dogma they were asked to accept in childhood. Reasonable men in the age of science could not be expected to believe anything they could not prove.

In that first sermon at the Belmont, as I have said, there were one thousand four hundred and eighty-eight empty seats. But, there were also one hundred and twelve seats with people in them—a small, alert audience seeking a workable philosophy; seeking proof. And I was a thoroughly convinced young man ready to present a series of phenomenal "coincidences" which went beyond the mathematical possibility of chance.

There had been, for instance, the cowboy. He was known to students at the Institute as Sagebrush Sam—his real name has long been forgotten. But he turned up out of Wyoming when I was first there as a student and what happened to him and the people around him became an evidential.

To put it kindly, Sam was unsavory. Out in the far gullies of the cattle country a jawbreaking chaw of tobacco is socially acceptable and there are few gentle lady practitioners to check up on how often you shave or bathe. Not so at the Institute. Sam wore a tobacco-stained walrus mustache, and his neck and ears were not regularly subjected to soap and water. A charming elderly lady, who was studying to be a practicing Christian, once characterized him as a mountain goat.

One day in the autumn Sam came tromping down Sixth Street, not in chaps, not in cowboy riding boots, but in faded blue jeans, a zipper jacket stained by exertions at the roundup, and heavy mail-order shoes. At the Institute steps he took a soiled copy of *Science of Mind* magazine from his hip pocket and verified the address. He had arrived that morning on a cattle train, and you didn't have to be a graduate criminologist to deduce it. He stalked in to register, and it was as if he traveled in a cloud.

"Ma'am," he told the girl at the desk, "I want to learn all about this here Science of Mind." He opened a checkbook and took out a gold-capped fountain pen. "How much?"

The girl hastened away to consult Ernest. She might have known. A cowboy? He was charmed and came out at once to make Sam welcome. Ernest had always been interested in unusual characters and Sam, obviously, was a prize.

The semester had begun, but Sam was sharp as a stiletto

and caught on at once. With jaws working and cheek gradually filling up, he sat at the back of the classroom near an easily opened door leading out on the fire escape. From his first day he became an island (there were always empty seats around him, front, back, and on either side). About four times an hour his bulging cheek forced him to the fire escape. It was thirty feet up, over a walkway, and Sam always had the politeness to peer in both directions before he fired; but the moist explosion was unmistakable and many a gentlewoman was properly offended. Even down in front, with our backs turned, all thought was suspended until Sam had regained his chair.

He was snubbed, of course. Or, perhaps, ignored is the word. More of the men might have sought him out if he had matched anybody's idea of a cowboy. We were familiar with the spruce Hollywood buckaroos, but Sam was a real cowboy, that was the trouble. During the class intermissions, avoided by all, he would lean against the wall, under a good light, thumb the textbook, and chaw. That folks hereabouts weren't too friendly didn't disturb him a mite. He hadn't come to Los Angeles to make friends, y'see. He'd come to find out how to heal. And not people, either. Cattle.

"Got some poorly cows up where I come from, Doc," he told Ernest. "Our vet has rode out six-seven times, tried six-seven wonder drugs and sends his bills regular, but we don't get *cures*. We got good grass and spring water and them animals oughta have shiny coats and the joy o' livin', but seems like they keep goin' down and down. Well, sir, one day in town, I find this here *Science of Mind* magazine. I took it home to the ranch and studied every doggone article in it. It makes sense, Doc. I seen wonders, m'self, in my day, but I didn't know about the *technical,* y'might say. So I come down here to learn it. I done well in school, whenever I went, and I think I can pick this up pretty good."

And he did pick it up pretty good. Nobody was better. We often sensed a smile under the walrus mustache when he could answer questions which the offended lady practitioners-to-be had missed.

Then came the proof. One night, toward the end of the first semester, the classroom filled up with visitors. Seats around Sagebrush Sam were taken by strangers until only one, the chair on his right, remained empty. As the class was beginning, a lady from the suburbs, one of the regulars, stood in the doorway looking around frantically. She was having a bad day, anyhow; her nose was red and she carried a box of tissues and was sucking a lozenge. Her cough was a horror, a racking, contralto bark. She came in with open reluctance. Chawing, Sam watched her without emotion. There was no other seat. The class began. She fluttered, sniffed haughtily, and sat down beside him.

And barked.

Chawing steadily, Sam cast a kindly eye upon her.

She barked again.

"Ma'am," he said, "looks like you could use a mite o' help. You want *me* to speak the Word?"

She was frightfully embarrassed, as she told us later, but for the first time she glanced past that stained mustache and into Sam's blue eyes. They were abrim with fellow feeling.

"Why, yes, please," she said miserably, and settled back. "Thank you."

Sam closed his eyes. His whisper was loud enough to disturb people four rows ahead.

Sam said: "There's a Universal Power which is also the

Power within; and this lady's cold is clearing up now as *I speak the Word. I* know an' *she* knows we can count on it. And so there is healing *right now*. And so it is."

It happened. It was flabbergasting. Only she could know for sure, only she could testify, but the astonishing change took place instantly; the tightness left her chest, the tickling vanished, she felt of her nose, her forehead, blinked in shock, and was well.

"Why–why–why, *thank you!*" she said, and stared at Sam in awe.

But it was time for Sam to step out on the fire escape. He stood up.

"I'm–I'm *healed!*" she cried, indicating that whereas previously she had hoped, now she believed. "Oh, thank you, Sam!"

"You're quite welcome, Ma'am," Sam said moistly, climbing over the nearby knees.

"Now I know!" the lady told the curious during intermission. "I've actually had it happen!"

Sam was modest. People clustered around him, but he said he hadn't done anything *they* couldn't do. The Power was universal. He was sure getting the idea, though, he told folks; he was getting what he'd come for.

People sought him out now. They even contested the adjoining chairs. "Want me to speak the Word, hey?" he would say to a sufferer. "Well, all right, now, settle back and *believe*." He warned: "Some folks won't let healing happen. You got to be willing to give up your cold or whatever illness you happen to be enjoying. And it's done *within*, y'know. You let health through, that's what you do."

Toward the end of the last semester he received a postcard from Wyoming and decided to go back home.

"But you won't graduate," I warned him. "Sam, a few more weeks and you'll have a certificate."

"Certificate!" he scoffed. "What cow is gonna care if I got a certificate! Man, I've got the *idea.* And that's what I come for—to get the technical planted solid in m'head, and prove it out. I done it and that's that."

Nobody at the Institute ever heard from him again. How the cattle are doing in Wyoming we wouldn't know, but of this we are sure: no cowboy in Sam's outfit who is willing to give up the cold will suffer long.

Ernest used Sam as an illustration in his teaching.

"The Law doesn't know about certificates, theological seminaries or dogma; the Law responded to Sagebrush Sam just as it will respond to you."

One Sunday morning, after Ernest had moved his own lectures to the Beverly, a sorrowing woman came belatedly into the almost-full theater and was ushered to the first row, where a single vacant seat remained. It was on the aisle next to an eleven-year-old boy. We never knew what grief she bore, but tears streamed down her cheeks as she tried to concentrate on Ernest's lecture. Finally, suppressing a sob with a convulsive breath, she buried her face in her hands. The boy gently touched her sleeve.

"Would you like *me* to speak the Word?" he whispered.

She saw an earnest, confident young face and real compassion.

"Why, yes," she said, and dried her eyes.

The boy folded his fingers and ducked his head; his lips moved.

Later, she told Ernest Holmes: "Only *I* can know the

peace that came over me. It was mystic. It was a balm. My grief was more than I could abide when I came to your service that morning. I can face the future now."

The boy, like Sagebrush Sam, had believed. Elsewhere, in some detail, we discuss Dr. Alexis Carrel's investigation of the medically attested healings at Lourdes, some of which are called "instant." For the moment, let us remark that Dr. Carrel found one consistent factor: somebody has to pray. Somebody has to believe. And not necessarily the patient.

One summer at Asilomar, after his morning lecture, Ernest and I walked miles to a restaurant near Pacific Grove. A surf running in Monterey Bay carried a sweeping inshore tide from the rocks at Lover's Point to the shallows of a sandy beach, a perfect run for surfboard enthusiasts. There were a dozen young men riding the breakers, indifferent to the chill of those glacial waters. We watched for an hour, talked to them about the sport and later, in Hawaii, I tried it myself.

The successful conclusion of the ride is implicit in a single early moment: when the rider first stands in perfect balance, catching the crest of the wave, aware of silence broken only by the whispering of the spray behind him, then, with the certainty of his perfect timing, he experiences a sense of total accomplishment. "I've done it!" he thinks, and from that moment the ride is all of a piece; it has already been accomplished, the beginning, the middle and the end.

This is what is meant by "believing."

When I arrived at the Belmont Theater that first Sunday morning, entering from the alley, through the stage door, I was met cheerfully by a man who had no legs. He was

Marty, the caretaker. He moved about nimbly on a little platform, propelling himself with padded blocks, one in each hand.

"Good morning, Reverend Hornaday," he beamed. "You're going to have a great success."

This was not merely opening-day best wishes. He had no doubt. I was grateful. He had struck the proper note for a first morning and we talked quietly for a few minutes. Marty didn't miss his legs, so I didn't either. I never again thought of him as being handicapped. When, weeks later, we were forced to move to a larger theater, I urged him to go along. But he said he had obligations at the Belmont. Wonderful things had happened to him there.

I had prepared a sermon based on something Ernest had said over lunch one day. When the mood was on him, Ernest was capable of platform rhetoric across a cottage cheese salad. After lunch I wrote down what I could remember in my notebook.

It went like this: In this amazing century, bursting away from so much that was slow-paced and orderly in the past, the breakthrough in the physical sciences robbed many people of cherished religious concepts and left them forlorn. But man is a religious being and there are thousands who are seeking a philosophy which can be reconciled to their own expanding awareness of the universe—a faith that will square with the century.

"Can you imagine a Nobel Prize winner holding still for an hour's talk on original sin?" he demanded. "No, people want the religion that Jesus brought to the world—if we can get back to it, through all the ecclesiastical forms. People who have left their churches to follow the mechanists have lost more than they can afford to lose. They're going to keep looking until they find a religion they can test, and prove out, and depend on."

That first Sunday morning I had planned to quote Pasteur who said:

"A little science estranges man from God, but much science brings him back."

Now, after the years between, I'm not sure I ever got around to quoting him. Just as I faced the audience, the podium lights went out. My notes vanished in the gloom. But it didn't matter. There were still fringe areas of doubt in my mind—that prayer could win a response from plants, for instance—but these were the most minor reservations. The would-be missionary who had lost his vocation had found it again; the weeks of association with Ernest and the practitioners and teachers at the Institute, the tales told by my fellow students, the healings witnessed with my own eyes, the happiness of Ernest's congregation before and after church, had given me what I sought, and I was eager to share it.

Mine was not a lecture; I preached a sermon. How could I do anything else? And the conditioning I'd received as a young man, offering the old theology in half-filled churches, had prepared me for the acres of empty seats at the Belmont. I'd heard my voice echo into emptiness often enough before. But then I hadn't known that a Law existed which my one hundred and twelve auditors and I could use, right then, and tomorrow, and forever. I told them about Ernest Holmes' first discovery of the healing factor of the Power within, and about my own experience in a Buddhist home, and what had happened to me since. It was a marshaling of proofs; they were presented that morning for examination.

The simple tale of Ernest's first enlightenment made an

impression, I remember. People talked about it afterward.

We all suspect that there are times when we have an emotional need for a cold. A flash of anger, of fear, envy, guilt, hurt feelings—and the next thing you know, you're sniffling. It's as if we said: I'm hurt but I'm too old to weep; I shall merely sniffle. At any rate, and for whatever reason, Ernest, when a boy in his teens, had been sent to bed with a sore throat. Mother Holmes had suggested that he read the Bible, but there was schoolwork to do and so he picked up a book by Ralph Waldo Emerson. He read the essay on Self-Reliance—and it changed his life. And mine. And, possibly, yours.

That magnificent essay burst upon the boy in concepts which would never leave him. He sat up straight and read:

> A man should learn to detect and watch that gleam of light which flashes across his mind from within, more than the lustre of the firmament of bards and sages. Yet he dismisses without notice his thought, because it is his. In every work of genius we recognize our own rejected thoughts; they come back to us with a certain alienated majesty.

A realization of the Power Within swept over him, and he reread the essay; and this time when he finished he was supremely confident of his own dominion. And with that belief came an instant healing. His sore throat was gone. Excitedly he ran to his mother. She felt of his forehead, thumped and examined—and agreed. And thereupon the search for a new philosophy began. There were the inevitable setbacks, but the evidentials multiplied, and before long he was a man with a message and a compulsion to share it.

When that first Sunday service was over, I left the stage

to greet the congregation at the door. I passed the head usher, who told me the amount of the morning offering. It was small. I visualized the figures $6,000 and tried to achieve the surfer's confidence as he stands in perfect timing riding the crest of the wave. It was not the moment for it.

An elderly gentleman had lingered after everyone else had gone.

"I'm Joe Bassett," he said, offering his hand. "Give Ernest Holmes my regards, Reverend. Beverly Hills is pretty far away for me these days. I knew Ernest when he'd bogged down and was a purchasing agent for the city of Venice."

I'd heard something about this. But Ernest, by now, was so firmly established as Dean and Founder of the Institute that it was difficult to think of him as working anywhere else.

"In the early days, after long and disciplined study, young Ernest Holmes opened an office as a spiritual counselor—but nobody came," Joe Bassett said. "Ernest sat there for months, y'know. Nothing happened. Then all of a sudden he found the key. You ought to hear the whole story if you're going to preach for him, young fellow. Get him to tell you."

He assured me that I'd have a bigger crowd next Sunday and so departed.

There were sounds of runners on the tile, and my friend the caretaker came scooting across the lobby.

"You'll have five hundred people next week, and double it before the month is out," he predicted. "That talk was a help to me, and I'm the average man."

Uplifted by the "taffy" from those generous people, I

drove to Ernest's house on Norton Avenue. He had other things on his mind, and my report didn't interest him right then. Earlier that morning Hazel had intercepted him in the front hall on his way to the theater and had forced him into black shoes with laces. He had just gotten home and was now wasting no time getting into the loafers. He did this by pressing the toe of one shoe against the heel of the other, thus slipping his foot out while leaving the loathed laces tied. With a happy sigh he stepped into the roomy loafers and nudged the shoes into the front hall closet.

"I got a laugh this morning that went crashing from the pit to the gallery," he told me. "What were you saying, Bill? How did you do?"

"The crowd was small, and so was the offering, but it's going to be all right," I told him.

He didn't need to hear it from me; he knew it was going to be all right. He had treated for this. He had prayed for this in his own affirmative fashion.

"I wasn't trying for a laugh. But it suddenly struck me. A man suffers the consequences of his own thinking and behavior, we *know* that, so we're the only church you'll find anywhere on the planet without a long list of do's or don'ts. This makes us the only church with no hypocrites in it." I smiled; he was disappointed. "Guess it's funnier from the platform," he said, and studied me. "Yes, you look all right. Look as if you could bear the consequences of your thinking."

"Next week I'm going to announce that we need six thousand dollars," I said. "I plan simply to announce it—and leave it there. I'll speak the Word."

"Say it once and let it go to work," he assured me comfortably. "That's what I always do!"

I wondered what was keeping him in the living room. Usually, after his Sunday lecture, he repaired at once to the kitchen where he put on a white apron and stormed the refrigerator. He could be a master chef when the mood was on him; even in hurried moments he was a sandwich maker much given to triple-deckers filled with surprises. He worked best with time to spare and condiments and cold cuts spread out on the counter. I told him about Joe Bassett.

"Joe Bassett!" he said, with a glance at the clock. "Joe took care of the trees along the parkway, a very important job. Oh, yes; good old Joe. Did he tell you how I met him?"

"He hinted at it."

"It's no secret. I've told it from the platform."

By the time he had opened his first office as a spiritual counselor, Ernest was sure that his philosophy was sound. He had witnessed scores of healings—dissolved many a stubborn problem—demonstrated abundance. The philosophy had been tested, and he believed. Yet, once established in the office, not even former students sought him out. He sat alone, with hours to devote to study. Weeks, then months, went by. Eventually, he closed the office and, through a friend of the family, got the job as purchasing agent. He needed time to think. With the philosophy proved by so many demonstrations, he knew that he himself somehow had failed.

"Now, pay attention to this, Bill," he said. "This should influence your attitude toward the problem you've got at the Belmont. It's a money problem. But if you dwell on money, and the need for it, and how it will affect you, you'll find yourself in the same box I got into."

One noon he had taken his lunch to a nearby city park. He was reading Thomas Troward's *Edinburgh Lectures* when a question popped into his mind which had to be faced: what had been his motive? When he had opened his office as a counselor, had he wanted to help people—or earn a living in congenial work?

This was a universe of law, a moral universe; it was important to know which had been first in his mind.

In truth, he had wanted a congenial way of life.

Wasn't that it?

Thoughtfully, he went back to the office. Obviously a clarification of motives was needed here. Had he now changed his emphasis? He was sure he had. He'd been praying for people in his own fashion, and in secret, all these months. Lately, friends and acquaintances again had been turning to him for help.

Occupied now with office chores, he neglected to put the Troward book away. Later in the afternoon the superintendent of streets came in with orders. He noticed the book, picked it up and skimmed a few pages. Judge Troward had been an intelligent man, a sound and lucid writer, and the superintendent, an engineer, found the book appealing. Ernest urged him to take it home.

He did. The ideas excited him and he read it avidly. Several times he consulted Ernest on points he hadn't understood and when, presently, he returned the book, he was enthusiastic.

"Look here, Ernest, suppose I invited a few friends over to the house some evening," he suggested. "People are searching, you know—we've been blown around like weather vanes lately. Will you talk to them?"

It was the beginning. The group enlarged with each

meeting. Soon, one of its members surprised even herself by engaging a hall for Sunday morning lectures. She had seen a sign: HALL FOR RENT and impulsively had gone in to make a deposit—because so many of her friends wanted to hear about the new philosophy. It seemed a proper working of the Law. Within two years from the time he clarified his motives—and with never an announcement or an advertisement in the newspapers—Ernest Holmes was speaking to twenty-five hundred to three thousand people each week.

"Never strain for a demonstration," he told me that first Sunday morning. "Let it flow. If you'll grant the basic assumption that we're part of the Universal Mind, then action in your own mind upon the Cosmos invites reaction. It is simple. But you have to understand it. And you have to believe it to be true. Then, under the Law of Mind in Action, ideas are brought into play which are made manifest in our experience. I'll tell you about another engineer who believed this, and *knows* it works. Joseph Straus who built the Golden Gate Bridge. Earlier attempts to sink pilings had to be abandoned, you know. They washed out in those fierce tides. Mr. Straus told me, himself, that he'd take the daily meditations from *Science of Mind* magazine with him when he went to work in the morning—"

Hazel called from the head of the stairs.

"Papa? Are you dressed? It's one-thirty. We should be there."

"Anytime," he said comfortably. "I'm ready, Hazel."

"Papa?"

He looked at me bleakly, knew what was coming.

"What shoes are you wearing?"

Silence. I got up and prepared to leave.

"Papa? Have you got the loafers back on?"

He was rebellious.

"They didn't invite us to lunch to inspect my shoes," he insisted.

There was an amiable little argument which he lost. We moved to the front hall. Hazel, satisfied now, waved to me and disappeared. The philosopher calmly slipped out of the loafers, slid them into the closet, and stood in his stocking feet surveying the hated laces which, of course, were tied. He wouldn't have time to tell me about Mr. Straus, he said glumly. Remind him some other day.

The laces on the right shoe were in a double knot. He struggled briefly.

"You're a string, not a knot," he said sharply. "Loosen up."

It loosened up.

He didn't have any trouble with the other one either.

"I'll be in the car!" he called up the stairwell. We went out. I'd been aware of a car with a temporary license when I drove up. The latest acquisition was longer and more luxurious than the old one. Affluence, I thought. Abundance. Law of Supply.

What a far cry from the fund-raising campaigns of my boyhood! Hazel came out and joined him and as they drove away I stood on the curb, watching the receding gleam, thinking of my Dad as I once had discovered him, aloft repairing shingles, roped to the church steeple, because the church couldn't afford to hire a steeplejack. He had called down reassuringly to the small figure of my worrying mother on the ground below.

There was never abundance in Dad's religion—but there was love, and faith sufficient to provide our daily bread.

There had been kindly members of the congregation—even one who had given them a vacation at Yosemite—but never prosperity, only small change in the collection plate often given by people as poor as we.

Times when I had substituted for an absent usher, hearing the thin tinkle of dimes and nickels, I'd wonder why God withheld so much from so many of His churches, from splendid people like my Dad and Mother. There had been wealth in every town to which we'd been assigned—but very little of it spilled over upon the true and dedicated servants of God. The problem had bothered me bitterly in my adolescence. Could this be the Lord's design, I asked—plenty for the godless on earth, the gentle whir of wings for the faithful in heaven? Were we, somehow, forever sinning? The rewards didn't square with the concept of a just God.

Recalling a hand-me-down blue jacket, the top feature in my hand-me-down wardrobe, I remembered a boyhood friend, an Episcopal rector's son, who never forgot the public humiliation he had suffered when the blue serge suit he wore to a church supper had been loudly recognized by its original owner, the Mayor's boy. My friend developed into the most grimly ambitious man I ever knew. He became a popular playwright with a compulsion toward public display of opulence. One night, after visiting with us, he stepped in behind his twelve cylinders to drive away and said: "My Dad prayed by rote to a God who never existed. But now, without a religion to hamper me, I've done all right."

He had used his great gifts with a shrewd eye to the box office; his family was still receiving royalties long after his suicide.

Agreed, then: his father had prayed to a God who never existed; but Ernest, embracing life and the universe, counseling of Love and Law, had found a God who did.

As you believe, so it is.

One morning when I stopped in at the Norton Avenue house for coffee on my way to the office, he greeted me from behind the open pages of the *Wall Street Journal.*

He folded the paper, called his broker, and bid on some blue chip stock. "Now, then. That's the end of my business day. How's the philosophy going, Bill?"

When I came into the Belmont through the stage door that second Sunday, my cheerful friend wheeled his platform swiftly across to me.

"Four hundred and eighty last time I counted," he said happily. "Remember what I told you, Reverend?"

We moved to the wings. The front rows were filling up. We listened.

The music had theme and melody. The organist had selected hymns to quicken the pulse, to brighten the mood. It had called for research, but he had managed to find cheerful hymns.

Can you afford the consequences of the way you are thinking? Ernest had asked.

This Sunday I could.

The theater has a harsh word for actors who draw too much satisfaction from their own performances: *ham.* And ministers, in their franker moments with their peers, will confess that it is easier to lose perspective in the pulpit than on the stage. Week after week the preacher steps out before rows of intent faces, bowed heads, eyes closed in prayer; and he must take care not to allow himself to utter, on his own authority, what he mistakes for the very word of God. For then, for sure, the Power within the listeners will measure him for what he is. I tried to remember, on this second Sunday morning, that what these listeners of mine wanted was a measure of what I myself was finding: proof.

We had the proofs in abundance. Here was one:

A little boy had a condition diagnosed as malignant. The doctors told the family they must abandon hope. Our congregation in Beverly Hills had treated for him. In his home a few blocks away the child brightened almost at once. He was taken back to the hospital. More tests, more X rays, and cheers.

A mistaken diagnosis, the doctors said.

There was a Law in operation, and there were techniques to which the Law responded. . . .

And then, as the soloist stood to sing the offertory anthem, I made my public affirmation.

"This is definite, and now affirmed," I said. "Six thousand dollars is needed for the basic operation of the Belmont's Sunday morning services. It is now forthcoming. . . ."

Along with all else I felt, as I shook hands with the congregation, there was profound gratitude. Churches had been my life; this was a new dimension, but once again I was a minister, and those two devout people, my parents, would have been pleased to find me there.

A lady wearing a small white turban offered an attractive smile and a firm gloved hand. She said something about a husband who had attended last Sunday and was ill today. She asked me to treat for him and I promised to do so.

"Your church is convenient for us, Reverend Hornaday. We will be proud to give the six thousand dollars you need. Shall I send the check to you at the Institute?"

There's a stage direction called double-take. Screen writers employ the words to guide the actors; it calls for a perfectly timed portrayal of belated reaction to news just past. An Irish comedian named Edgar Kennedy was said to have been the originator of the double-take. He maintained a bland expression until the audience had recovered from its own shock—whereupon his tardy surprise rocked the rafters.

The lady in the white turban was laughing at me. Afraid of public thanks, she briefly laid a finger against her lips.

"The check will come from Philip and Amy Prior," she whispered. "It will be at the Institute tomorrow."

She hurried away; the rest was euphoria.

So soon! It was overwhelming.

It was loaves and fishes.

A few minutes later I was in my car, hurrying to Norton Avenue and Ernest's house. Lena took her time about answering the door. Doctor and Mrs. Holmes had gone to Santa Monica, she told me. Dr. Holmes was conducting a wedding this afternoon.

I decided to save the news for Monday morning. I would stroll into the office and casually toss the check on Ernest's desk. *Fait accompli*—this was always best.

Odd, wasn't it?—never for a moment did I doubt that the check would come.

6

Proofs—and Galley Proofs

> All things and events are rooted in a coordinated and intelligent principle which we call "divine." Any name limits it. God is in and through all life, the cause back of it, the effect in it, the power through it, the law sustaining it, the unity binding it together. Our lives are rooted in this unity and our relationship to it is instantaneous and mutual.
>
> —ERNEST HOLMES

The *Fish Bowl* was the staff's name for my office. Two steps up and there I was with aquarium privacy in a glass room six-by-eight with sunny California beaming on me from two sides. But it was the cool of the morning on Monday when I arrived to open the mail. I shuffled through twice before I found it: a neat white envelope from the Chapman Park Hotel. It turned up near the bottom of the stack. The note said:

Dear Reverend Hornaday:

For a very special reason which he will explain to you later, Philip has long wished to make a generous contribution as a tangible expression of gratitude for all that Dr. Holmes' philosophy has done for him. Our check is enclosed. Philip's health is much improved and we look forward to hearing your lecture next Sunday.

Sincerely,
Amy Prior

I was out of the Fish Bowl and halfway down the hall before I remembered to saunter. Ernest's office door was closed. His secretary plunged in from somewhere and jerked my arm away as I lifted my fist to knock. She looked harried for so early in the morning.

"Oh, no! Stay out, Bill."

"What's wrong?"

"Galleys—the new galleys." She remembered to lower her voice. "Ernest can't be disturbed by anybody for any reason. Go away."

"But I've got a check for six thousand dollars—"

"I don't care if it's a million. You know what he's like when he's reading galleys."

I didn't know. I hadn't been there long enough. But I soon found out. Ernest, always the philosopher, with a talent for detaching himself from the problem and treating for it, nevertheless was not at his balanced best when reading galleys.

"What's going on out here?"

His door had opened. His gray hair looked as if he'd just had both hands in it.

The secretary disappeared and, caught without words, I stood with the check concealed behind me.

There was a general brightening.

"Come in, Bill," he said, with unexpected warmth. "Come in and close the door."

I sauntered in and closed it. As he moved around to his big chair I said casually:

"By the way, Amy and Philip Prior—do the names mean anything to you?"

He fussed with the galleys. Half a dozen stub pencils were on the blotter. Ernest probably never used a whole pencil in his life. Thrift led him to salvage stubs which other people had discarded.

The next thing I knew the pencils were bouncing.

"I'm wrong!" he said, hammering the desk with both fists. "I *have* to be wrong. The fact that you and I have not yet reached our highest concept of normality points to the thought that there is an ideal man seeking emergence through us. Right?"

"I'm perfectly normal this morning," I said, defensively.

He wasn't listening. "Even people who are outwardly normal have times when they are not. Right, Bill? Have you ever met a man you considered to be perfectly happy? I have. But you've never met anybody, and neither have I, who doesn't sometimes become discouraged. Isn't that true?" He slammed an open palm on the galleys. "Every time, every blessed time I get a batch of these things I have to fight a compulsion to rewrite 'em."

He'd stopped for a breath, so I tossed the check on his desk. Lying there on top of the galleys, it looked as good as money to me—commercial size, numbered, with the name and address of the Priors printed on it.

"Kindly take a look at that and cheer up," I said.

"Um?" He bent over and peered. "Well, well, that's fine. That's the Law in Action, y'see?" He read Amy Prior's letter and admired the quality of the hotel's paper.

It was hard to get his attention back to the miracle.

"Philip Prior apparently understands something you once wrote," I told him. "Maybe it's something you read in galleys long ago—and wanted to rewrite."

"Write 'em a warm letter," he said. "They'll want something explicit for their tax man." I'd been right. There *was* a general brightening. A beautiful calm was settling on him. "Bill, have you ever read galleys—know anything about it?"

"No. No, I really don't."

"Simple matter, you'll pick it up fast." He swung his feet down and fumbled through the desk drawer until he'd found a chart. "Here's a guide for the proper proof marks. Dodd, Mead sent it, um? Read the galleys for me, will you, Bill? If I'm too abstract, or sentences get too wordy—" He dwindled off and glanced at his watch. "Read, say, until ten o'clock and then we'll go for a walk."

The staff called them "Meditation Walks," though he did precious little meditating along the way. He would accost strangers with shopping bags and ask them what they thought of prices—and then point out to me afterward the danger of bitterness. "How are *you* doing these days?" he might say to a well-dressed man waiting for the light to change. Tidy babies in prams all but undid him, and they would respond to him as if he were Santa Claus with a bagful of gifts. So would cats. So would dogs. So, I found out later, would trees and flowers. There was intelligence everywhere in nature, there was consciousness in everything, he said, and he wasn't above talking things over with a thirsty tree on a busy street.

All this and galleys, too.

He beamed at me, picked up the morning paper, and I went out.

The comptroller accepted the Priors' check without comment. When I dictated a lengthy, heartfelt letter which the Priors might show to the tax man, the secretary was unmoved. Hazel Holmes had just arrived in her own nearby office, so I went in and told her about it. She, too, listened calmly as she peeled off her gloves.

I exploded. "Everybody around here acts as if six thousand dollars came in every Monday morning," I said. "And to me this is earth-shaking! One affirmation—and an instant reaction. Is this just routine?"

It took more than this to disturb her serenity.

"There are times, William, when money is desperately needed," she said, hanging up her coat. "But there *is* a Law of Mind in Action, there *is* abundance, and the money *does* come."

My slide off cloud nine had ended at this point and I found myself alone in the hall, closing her door. Into the anticlimax as I settled down in the Fish Bowl to read galleys came memories of my dad; never in the fifty years of his ministry had there been a time when the strain had been eased. The trip to Yosemite had been a holiday from the financial problems which still awaited his return; all his life he had been generous, devout—and poor. Never a time when the Law of abundance had gone into action for him. Nor was that all. Like many another minister, he couldn't be sure, even in the happier assignments, that a petition was not being circulated because somebody in the congregation wanted a younger man. Or one less fundamental. Or one less liberal. Or one without four children. Yet, in spite of the threadbare aspects of his ministry, there had been magnificent achievements. There was a sturdy monument in Nevada—and we could point to that.

When assigned to a little church in Carson City, the year I was born, Dad discovered that prisoners in the State Penitentiary were being punished on the rock pile—days, weeks, months, years spent in meaningless hard labor. He persuaded Governor Boyle and the warden to allow the men to build a stone church.

The men welcomed the idea, and the job was done with pride and skill and gratitude—well, yes, with love. "Why, we've got all the time in the world!" was a joke that never failed when the craftsmen worked to get an exact level. The beautiful stone church exists to this day. Dad had turned an idea into a lasting expression, bound a period of his life in stone.

There were other values just as lasting. Among us, his children, there had been a cheerful acceptance of the harsh facts of life. From the beginning we understood that we four would go to college, and graduate, and earn our way. We were taught skills. Three of us learned to play musical instruments. In the course of becoming an attorney—and he became a distinguished one—my brother took any odd job that came along. One sister became a professional harpist, another a pianist and an art-and-music teacher in the public schools. My own marimba took me to the Orient and back, my first trip, when I was a high-school sophomore—sixteen, but tall enough and venturesome enough to exaggerate my age. A compulsion to succeed was characteristic of the ministers' children I knew in the various towns of my youth. Perhaps lack, self-discipline and a sense of moral values laid a sound foundation for later achievement. *Who's Who,* I'm told, lists a predominant number of the sons and daughters of ministers and rabbis among its notables.

So it was with a sigh for Dad's hard years that I turned

at last to the proofs. And here was Ernest Holmes on "Immortality," no equivocation, either.

"Immortality means a continuation of the individual stream of consciousness beyond physical disintegration," he wrote. "The fact, as reported, of the resurrection of Jesus has been the hope of millions for centuries; yet there are those who question the records and doubt that such a man as Jesus ever lived. But one thing is certain. The average human desires to live beyond the grave. All, or almost all, abhor the thought of oblivion. Even in the tensions of life, people still believe in life. On Easter both the spring hats and the hopeful faces give evidence that, though they may not care much for churches as a regular thing, or sermons, it's still a believing world." He insisted that such a universal belief had a basis in reality: *"It seems to me there is an intuitive something in us that knows. Just as we know that we now live, we know that we shall keep on living."*

Every new encounter with Ernest's thinking broadened the scope of my own; and those words thrilled me. He had devoted years of scholarship, at the height of his career, to the examination of a belief that is implicit in all men—implicit, he said, until blurred by a world that is too much with us. His search led him to the acceptance of immortality, a concept which he never lost for a moment, not even at the time of Hazel's passing, not even on his own last day. He said: Some inner *I* tells us, even in times of disaster, that all is well.

A man he knew had been carried to the very edge of the abyss and, returning to consciousness, found himself under an oxygen tent—but in such peace of mind that he could say, calmly: "Whatever happens will be all right, Ernest. I have seen the glory of God and all is well."

Many children, perhaps all, are born with a sense of continuity; in our earliest memories, we see ourselves as *being*, without beginning and without end. Children recover from the shocks. Old people die. A kitten dies. A puppy dies. A bird flies blindly against the windowpane and dies. There is grieving for small pets. Then, unaccountably, unjustly, a child dies and the horror of death becomes part of another child's life. Yet it is a rare individual who expects to lose his own continuity. There are intellectuals in their middle years who tell you how they'll welcome the endless sleep; but subsequent behavior too often reveals that they, too, accept endings for others, not for themselves. All of us, in health or illness, are aware of an inner, intact core, the observant *I*. You will live forever, Ernest had written boldly. It was his deepest belief. It is threaded through his philosophy, through all his books and lectures. And, reading his words now, I could—with joy—release my devoted parents to a new dimension, whatever it might be, and carry on the family tradition in the complete freedom of a new philosophy—new, but still as old as time.

A phrase from the galleys struck me sharply—an *unlived life*.

One of my fellow students at the Institute recently had told me that she was living in a state of gradual awakening. I knew what she meant.

Ernest pointed out that people wore labels. Mine was: *waking up!* Coming back from a walk, he loved to sit on the steps at the Institute and watch the parade on Sixth Street. *What's her label?* he would say. *What's his?* Attitudes of mind might well have been printed on framed placards and worn about the neck: MARTYR: or—PERSECUTED; REJECTED; NO HOPE; BUSYBODY; GUILT; I CAN SELL ANYTHING; DON'T ASK ME, I DON'T KNOW; JUST MY LUCK; WHAT'S THE USE; or—GOLLY, WHAT A LOVELY DAY.

Each in his own world, a world created by his own thinking.

There would be dialogue as we sat on the steps.

HORNADAY: Even after studying the labels you believe that man himself offers positive proof that God *is*?

HOLMES: I do. However, I believe the life principle is greater than what it creates, though creation is its activity, and this activity takes place through involution and evolution. I think the activity of life-principle is for the purpose of self-expression.

HORNADAY: Even the man who went by here labeled *martyr*?

HOLMES: He was enjoying it. There are magnificent areas he may move into later, but at the moment he has chosen martyrdom. That's *his* business. (Pause.) I don't see how we could have any genuine experience without will and choice, do you, Bill?

HORNADAY: No.

HOLMES: And once we grant will and choice, we must admit the possibility of dual experience.

HORNADAY: I'm not sure of your meaning. Are you talking about good and evil?

HOLMES: I'm willing to ponder it.

HORNADAY: Nobody has ever solved that one.

HOLMES: I'll say this: we can't judge everything from a few experiences. Nor can we judge man's possibilities by viewing him from the cradle to the grave. I assume that if we could see the ultimate, we would understand what now seems inexplicable. My study has forced me to believe that man has within him the latent possibility of freedom, joy, completion. All of us are born with the capacity to learn more than we ever do learn, achieve more than we ever do achieve—man has limitless if undeveloped possibilities.

HORNADAY: But you haven't begun to discuss good and evil.

HOLMES: I say that the Ultimate Intelligence knows neither good nor evil as we think of them. Our ideas about good and evil change rapidly. For me it comes to this: unless I were convinced of the continuation of my own existence I should view any present good as evil because I should be so torn by the realization that the good I now experience is soon to end—and I with it. I could not answer any questions about life unless I believed in an eternity in which I am included.

HORNADAY: Isn't that the small ego?

HOLMES: No, it is the eternal *I*.

HORNADAY: When you talk about man's limitless possibilities, you would claim then that each child is born perfect?

HOLMES: Spiritually perfect.

HORNADAY: What about a child born deaf, dumb and blind? Isn't that evil?

HOLMES: Evil takes on a different light when man sees himself as an eternal being. He will regain his faculties somewhere.

HORNADAY: That's not too heartening for someone who must spend most of a century in darkness and silence.

HOLMES: Perhaps he will evolve rapidly enough in other ways to compensate. You think at once of Helen Keller and the triumph of her intelligence.

HORNADAY: But how can you and I be at peace as long as other people on our earth are obliged to live in horror? A child is murdered. Dictators impose slavery on whole societies. How can we know comfort when other people's lives are tragic?

HOLMES: There is evidence that man is evolving. I look to the day when we overcome our experiences and rise triumphant over present limitations. There *are* mysteries—but now we know there is also Law. In order to abide here we must have a very positive acceptance of the ultimate goodness of life—toward which goodness I believe we are all traveling. We have will and choice in this life; but the Universal Intelligence must be the essence of goodness, beauty and truth.

HORNADAY: You may have come as close to an answer as we're likely to get this morning. It follows then that when a high I.Q. professor in a college offers his students a philosophy which reduces man to nothingness, he is guilty of a murderous disservice to the human race.

HOLMES (grabbing my arm): There goes a woman labeled *I am asleep*. You see a lot of that, um? The label says: *I move, live, procreate and die in my sleep. Mine is an unlived life*. Small trials have convinced her of the futility of life; something she has read, heard, accepted has convinced her of nothingness at the end and so, having embraced the ultimate negative, she goes through life in a trance. And it is sad. There are songs to be sung, a love to be expressed. There are lessons to learn. There is no end of time, of course, and we are forever in process, but since one must wake up and live eventually, how much wiser to wake up now.

HORNADAY: What we have said so far is this, then: in order to be happy and productive and reasonably comfortable on this mysterious planet we must believe in spiritual evolution, which is immortality.

HOLMES: Yes. Positively so. Bill, we have order, not chaos, in the cosmos. If man could wholly accept the concept of his own eternal evolving, we might then have order instead of chaos here on earth. It's basic. It's high time we enlarged our view.

In those days Ernest couldn't get enough of talk, or enough of people. His was an unhampered view of the passing scene. He had not had a full, academic education, but his knowledge was so vast and so explicit that he counted among his close friends many of the highly trained intellects of the day—and he more than held his own with them.

In his early years of study he haunted libraries, took home armloads of tomes, gleaned, made outlines, compared and weighed philosophies, searched up and down through the ages with an eager, open mind. When he encountered questions he couldn't answer, he sought out experts. And paid them for information—what he could afford, that is. Once the secretary of the head of the philosophy department of a state university was turning him away when the great man himself came in and listened with amusement. Ernest had offered to pay five dollars for the answers to five questions. Unlike the secretary, the department head considered this a reasonable offer, invited Ernest into his private office, listened to the questions, answered them and, at Ernest's insistence, pocketed the money. Thereafter it became the young scholar's policy to seek other sources for other views, and to pay his way. He read rapidly, absorbed what he read—his memory was phenomenal—and soon his industry and the scope of his work won the respect of many learned men who were delighted to help and guide him. It is doubtful if formal schooling could have provided him with the education he won for himself. That impressive hard-won union label, the Ph.D., so important to instructors, came to him later on in honorary degrees—as a matter of fact, universities all over the world honored him.

Once he gave the graduation address to a college of

physicians and surgeons and he brought the young men to their feet cheering. "You deal with an inner healing Power —and so do I," he told them. He described the wonders of the human body in their own terms—and in his; here were wonders beyond the possibility of accidental origin; his speech sang of his belief in an Ultimate Good, of God.

And so did the words I was now reading in the galleys: "We sense a divinity within, a nature hidden in the cryptic interior of our minds which we have scarcely penetrated—a unity with the Whole. The intuitive faculty which we use to uncover Reality is evidence that this Reality is already latent within us—"

"How about the walk, Bill?"

He had stuck his head in the door. He pretended indifference as I put the galleys in the middle drawer, but when we turned into the street and I complimented him on the clarity of his writing, there was once again a perceptible brightening. "Good, is it?" he asked, quickening his step. "Not flowery? Sometimes I get a bit carried away."

That was true enough. He was a sentimental man and he absorbed poetry through his pores. Apt quotations bubbled up in him, especially at christenings; whenever he took a baby in his arms, he was lost. The more beautiful the child, the more poetry he remembered, and the more abundant were the tears. "Have you *really* looked into these eyes?" he would ask the mother—when perhaps she was not yet steady on her feet after the ordeal in the hospital. "Have you noticed the quality of the blue, discovered the laughter and the sparkle, the incredible beauty here?" He saw more than most of us; saw in the child's blue eyes the Ultimate Goodness of God. Sometimes he got carried away at the end of a lecture when a theaterful of people had been especially attentive. One spring morning at the Ebell he closed thusly:

"Religion should be like the morning sun sending forth its rays of light; it should be like the falling dew covering the land with sweetness and fragrance, like the cool of the evening and the repose of night." Flowery? But hearing what had gone before, you knew that here was genius, too.

The morning walks provided an escape from the telephone. A philosopher who talks of healing to three thousand people every week is under endless pressure from the newcomers, who have not yet recognized that the healing Power is ever within themselves. "You can say I'm on a meditation walk," he would grin; he had to have time to think, and in my case, to teach. Often in the early years I'd write down whatever I could remember when we came back to the office. I find this note:

"Once upon a time everybody thought the earth was flat. That didn't flatten it. Then the time came when everybody knew it was a sphere. That didn't make it one; it had been this from the beginning, but now everybody's concept changed with the new discovery. As we better understand the immutable laws and the way they operate, the universe, to us, appears to change. We neither make nor change the truth. Think of creation as some effect of intelligence operating through law. Divine Principle is not God any more than electricity is God. It is a law of God. It is a mental law of cause and effect. When your thought is impressed upon it, it is its nature to take that thought and execute it exactly as you think it. If there is destruction in the thought, it must destroy. If there is good in the thought, it will execute goodness or healing."

Once, in the early days, he abruptly abandoned the lesson to commiserate with a cluster of sycamores in a neglected triangle of city park.

What was going on here, he demanded. Not watered, lately? And why not? He talked it over with the trees. "We'll invoke the law here, Bill," he told me, and caressed a tree in sympathy.

At such times I became a minister of the old school, not above disassociating myself by moving a few steps away. But he started to look for a hydrant, which seemed a reasonable procedure. "Intelligence in and through all life," he said, "is manifest in the sycamores and will respond when we speak the Word." He turned up evidence that the city engineers, in widening the street at this point, had torn out the sprinkler system and failed to replace it.

"Let us bless these trees, Bill," he said. "I affirm their right to food and water." He closed his eyes and continued in silence; then: "So it is!" He patted a dusty little tree branch: "Now, don't worry. The Word is in action. All will be well."

It is difficult now to recapture the skepticism which sometimes beset me. How sensible was this behavior of Ernest's—to bless a tree, affirm its right to food and water, pat it, talk to it, and walk on, dismissing the affirmation with an authoritative "So it is!"

After this incident I made a point of driving by the triangular parkway night and morning; it was only a mile off my regular daily route. Nothing happened. Five or six days, still nothing. Then, homeward bound one evening, I saw pipes laid out in the dried grass. The next morning I found several cheerful workmen digging a ditch near the dusty trees.

"Of course!" I thought. "Ernest probably called the street department."

That would be affirmative prayer in action in a perfectly reasonable fashion. No hocus-pocus about this. I decided to face him with it; and I did—almost.

He was in his office enjoying the morning mail. He always enjoyed the mail. Bills were a rarity. He believed in abundance, but he also believed in paying in cash. "Inasmuch as you're going to demonstrate abundance," he told his students, "demonstrate it in advance. It's no more difficult, and you save the interest."

"Those saplings on the city parkway," I began. "The street department is laying pipes, Ernest."

It was a moment before he remembered. Prayer acts independently after the prayer is prayed, he had said. He had detached himself from this one, sure enough.

"Oh, oh, yes—well, that's good, Bill. Yes, that's *good,* isn't it?"

There was innocent gratitude in his expression. Pure inspiration led me to maintain a golden silence. I went away with my questions unasked. Had he called the street department? I never knew.

But that was the first of many such incidents, and now here at my desk in Founder's Church, all these years later, I can look across to the glass partition which separates my office from the "Meditation Garden" and see a thriving tree which Ernest once rescued with the Word—a demonstration which I witnessed with my own eyes.

Amid the ferns and shrubs of the garden three small trees had been planted; two of them flourished, but the middle one languished from the beginning, lost its leaves and, the gardener reported, died. Early one morning Ernest and I were here in the office planning the dedication service when the gardener came through with a spade. He apologized for disturbing us.

"I've come for the dead tree," he said.

Ernest abandoned the conference and followed the gardener into the garden.

"Now hold on!" Ernest said, examined the tree and addressed it directly. "How will you ever find a better spot than a meditation garden?" he demanded, and proceeded to talk things over with the tree almost as if it were a heedless adolescent.

The gardener grinned in embarrassment.

"Did you plant it carefully?"

"Yes, sir, same as the others."

"Same food and water?"

"Yes, sir."

"Well, then, it's going to be all right." He told the tree to count its blessings! "There's love here," he explained. "Everybody's been pretty busy getting ready for the opening service, but you mustn't think you aren't admired." Then he made a long, silent affirmation. "It'll do fine now," he assured the gardener. "Leave it alone."

We watched the tree closely, the gardener and I. As this is written, it is taller than the other two and every bit as healthy.

Coincidence?

Memories come endlessly and, like folded tissues taken from a box, one produces another—and at what point, as Ernest often asked, do we go beyond the mathematical possibility of chance? In small matters and large ones, in desperate illness, in cases of financial need, he invoked healing with the absolute confidence that it would be accomplished. Usually it was. Not always—but often enough to be impressive.

Let's begin with an incredible incident. I won't ask you to believe it, but it must go into the record. Once again, with Bernard Opley, put it down to a coincidence and add a capital C if you like.

A slatternly woman in a housedress was hanging diapers on a clothesline at the back of a shabby, unkempt house as we walked by one day. A dirty youngster, lately in tears, sat nearby on a rusty tricycle, breathing convulsively, emotions spent. The place was a shambles. A torn curtain dangled in a side window; another open space was stuffed with cardboard; weeds grew on the driveway, paint was peeling off the house. Ernest stopped beside the picket fence. I said something about children inheriting adults' despair.

"We'll go to work on this," Ernest said firmly. The woman took the child and went up the sagging back steps into the kitchen. "Somebody needs help here. Let us bless this house and all who dwell therein."

"Maybe there's a landlord who doesn't care," I suggested.

"Then we'll bless the landlord."

Passers-by slowed their steps to stare at us. He was oblivious.

"All are members of One family," he said. "Whatever is needed by this household or the owners of this house, let it be fulfilled. Let there be an awakening to the Infinite harmony which guides and blesses everyone concerned." He plunged into a long, silent affirmation, concluding with a ringing *"So it is!"*

He was aglow with faith as we walked on. Faith? With conviction.

When I passed the house the next morning on my way to work—it was only six or seven blocks out of my way—I compared Ernest's prayer with the old theology supplications directed vaguely heavenward toward a moody, unpredictable Jehovah and decided that this, valid or not, was in all ways preferable; Ernest lived in a sweeter universe than the hardheaded mechanist who would scoff at him. And yet . . . Prayers to a moody Jehovah had gone winging into an empty sky; what about a silent affirmation spoken for strangers in a shabby house? Was it any more sensible? "We use our God-given power of choice," Ernest had said to me as we walked one morning. "We may choose whether to use the Law constructively or destructively. I have witnessed proof in hundreds of cases that *all is Love and yet all is Law in the realm of the mind.*"

Two weeks went by. Nothing happened. I waited until lunch one noon to report the failure. "You'd better treat again for that house, Ernest," I warned. "Nothing's changed."

He had brought along blank sheets from a yellow pad when we left the office and now was at work with a stub pencil writing busily.

"There's no need to do any more for that house, Bill," he said sharply. "It's already in action. Don't you understand? It's done. We affirmed it. And Something within me has said: 'It's done.' "

He wrote steadily for several minutes and then grinned at me.

"The publishers are bringing out the nineteenth printing of one of my books," he said. "It's thirty-five years since the first publication, and I've just written"—he read from the yellow sheet—"This much I know—that if I were writing this book today it would be penned with far greater conviction than it was thirty-five years ago. I have witnessed proof in these intervening years. I am more convinced than ever that Science of Mind, based upon the teachings of Jesus, and coordinated with the philosophy of other great thinkers of the ages, is destined to become the new religion for the new day."

He's willing to go right out on the limb, I thought.

At any rate, I was studying an open-end philosophy with a mentor who never blinked a question. The Day of Judgment and the Sound of Trumpets had gone glimmering for me, and good riddance, too; and Ernest's unwavering conviction was contagious. When he said: "I sincerely believe there are plantings in this world which can bear fruit only in another," a glimpse of infinite shining terraces came into my mind, a vision I've never lost. His approach was not exclusive. The Divine Principle was to be found in every sanctuary, every faith. What a hope for a chaotic world if all mankind found this to be a reasonable philosophy!

Reasonable. That was the key word. Ernest invited questions. Intelligent men and women should insist on proof, he said.

Then in the process of my own education Sagebrush Sam turned up, startled everybody, spoke the Word, got the response and disappeared. There were other Coincidences, and a whole new informal way of worship. Sometimes there was applause in the middle of sermons; always there were happy faces at the Sunday lectures.

I studied and watched and waited and learned.

Meanwhile my daylight travels took me past the forlorn house from day to day. An adult's despair was reflected in the pitiful remnants of the child's abandoned games. Discarded red-label soup cans. Dribbles of sand. The upended tricycle.

And then it happened!

One morning, about a month after Ernest's affirmation, I saw shingles being flipped off the roof of the old house as I drove by. Workmen swarmed about. I slammed on the brakes, skidded to the curb, and stared. Two Japanese gardeners were digging up the front lawn, preparing to plant sod and shrubbery. The slatternly woman could be seen washing windows inside. The tricycle was right side up this morning. The child was on the front steps playing with a roly-poly mongrel pup. A truck from the glass company stood in the driveway. The house, and its people, had suddenly come awake.

Whatever questions you have in your mind as you read were with me as I drove on. Houses often slip into disrepair, I thought. Neglected houses in good neighborhoods are to be seen every day, everywhere—and eventually somebody comes along to spruce them up. A coincidence? The normal turn of events?

Maybe so.

Yet what was happening to me? Dr. Ernest Holmes "treated" for a new assistant, a preacher, and a complex of forces lifted me out of an established business, where I was not happy, into the Institute and the Belmont, where I could use whatever talents I possessed—and every moment of my time. Coincidence? There had been Sagebrush Sam and a lady's startled, almost hysterical outburst: *"I'm healed!"* Not a coincidence. There'd been the saplings and the new pipes. Might have happened anyway. But in the continual hard study at the Institute more and more new, uplifting concepts engaged my mind until, now, in my own consciousness, I was moving into a vast new universe—with my outward world changing, too. How much more proof did I need? Would I forever follow the limping footsteps of the monk in the Middle Ages who, after praying until he could hardly bend his knees, was heard to say repeatedly: "I believe, help thou mine unbelief"?

The laws of the universe were never set aside to produce miracles, but with a new understanding of the *working* of the law one's own awareness changed and there were wonders to behold.

Was that it?

Yet the "miraculous" healings recorded by the unemotional Medical Bureau at Lourdes prompted Dr. Alexis Carrel to say: "Despite their small number they prove the existence of organic and mental processes that we do not know . . . The only condition indispensable to the occurrence of the phenomenon is prayer."

At Lourdes there had been medically attested instantaneous healings of malignancies—and apparently there was no need for the patient himself to pray, or even to have any religious faith.

But—and it's worth repeating—in every case there had been that one common factor: somebody had prayed.

Was that enough?

There was another question: what *sort* of prayer? The "miracle" cures had been few in number. Had the prayers in those cases been affirmations, wholly believed?

No question about Ernest; *he* believed.

"All are members of One family," he had declared that

first day we encountered the neglected house, and included a possible landlord in his blessing. "Whatever is needed—let it be fulfilled."

This time, I thought, I wouldn't rush into his office with heedless enthusiasm. Instead, I'd make a casual announcement over lunch at the club which I had joined when I was still a businessman. Ernest enjoyed the all-male atmosphere of the grillroom, the captain's chairs, the polished tables.

"Jonathan Club? Good," he'd say. "Delighted, Bill."

That noon he walked in beside me, beaming. All sorts of men gathered around him while he sipped Bristol Cream sherry. Yes, I know. Harvey's Bristol Cream is a dessert wine. But that's what he always ordered. One glass. Never more. And left some of it. To me it was always an endearing performance.

After he had accepted compliments from several businessmen who had heard him on a recent Sunday at the Beverly Theater, we ordered lunch.

"By the way," I said casually, "that house y'know, Ernest? Remind me to drive past it on the way home. They ought to have the new roof on by the time we get there. It's going to be beautiful."

There was weariness and wisdom in his glance.

"Bill, you have an ambivalent feeling about this," he decided. "Stop by that house and ask the people exactly what happened. Shred it down to the roots. Perhaps it *was* a coincidence."

"I'll build on the evidentials I *know* about," I said. "There's Sagebrush Sam. I've been eyewitness to the instant healing of the common cold."

"And missed the point," he grinned. "The important thing is the unsavory character of Sagebrush Sam. The law is no respecter of persons. It operates for the bathed and the unbathed alike."

What followed later on, after my second Sunday at the Belmont, would have been incredible if I hadn't lived through it—along with thousands of others who will remember when they read these words. The sort of thing which made Ernest the convinced man he was when I met him began happening to me. We outgrew one theater and then another: People came in desperation—and the wonders followed, and all in a perfectly natural way without golden stairs to heaven or the whir of wings; miracles that began *within*. For instance, there was the case of the ugly girl.

7

The Eye of the Beholder

> All men seek some relationship to the Universal Mind or the Eternal Spirit which we call God.
>
> —ERNEST HOLMES

During my second semester at the Institute, Ernest Holmes asked me to take over, during his holiday, the nightly radio program *This Thing Called Life.* When he returned in the fall, he was busy with a new book and so left me there. Now, almost two decades later, this rewarding challenge seems to be permanent. The program is heard in the western states just before midnight and is carried overseas by the Armed Forces Radio and Television Service. A producer at KFI recently told me we have twenty million listeners. Discount this any way you like and it's still a sobering responsibility.

The insomniac, the would-be suicide, the guilt-ridden, the disenchanted, those who are "mad at God," as well as those aware of an inner Power, tune in and, apparently, listen. More than a few phone the office for appointments to talk things over.

Time can be stretched, but still there are two sermons to be presented on Sunday, at nine-thirty and eleven, and another on Wednesday evening. There are teaching sessions, board meetings at the Institute, church correspondence, the five four-minute radio sermons to prepare and put on tape at the radio studio, and the marriages and baptisms and funerals. There are executive chores in a busy office—and, in a hidden-away house high in the hills near Pasadena, a generous and understanding family waiting dinner. No complaint, mind you—this is a rewarding way of life. But it creates appointment problems. We always have a waiting list of unhappy or desperate or grateful people.

Late one afternoon, when I was trying to crowd the writing of a broadcast into an odd half hour I'd found by accident, there was a brisk knock at my office door and Georgia, my secretary, popped in as if somebody were chasing her. She closed the door pointedly.

"Sorry," she said. "This girl hasn't an appointment, and I know you're busy—"

"What's her trouble?" I emerged slowly and put down my pencil.

"Poor thing. She must be the ugliest girl in the world," Georgia whispered.

"Is she a member of the church?"

"No. She heard your broadcast last night; apparently you said that every problem has an answer."

"That's true."

Georgia looked at me doubtfully. "Maybe so. But this one's the biggest challenge yet."

"Why, Georgia—I thought you'd joined up," I said.

When Georgia had come to work for us a few years before, we hadn't asked her church affiliation; we never do. There isn't anything that we believe which can't be accommodated in any other religion, unless you're splitting fine fundamentalist theological hairs, and what she believed didn't matter, because we knew for sure what *we* believed. And after she had been around for a time, she came into the office one morning wearing a white blouse with Aladdin's lamp cuff links and said she'd discovered what we meant when we said: *Use the lamp.* She hadn't yearned for a castle or diamonds or silver ice buckets, but she was now sure that every man had his own genie. She'd encountered her own in a family evidential beyond the mathematical possibility of chance.

But now she was afraid I'd gone too far.

"I'll bet she's suicidal, Dr. Bill," she said anxiously. *"I* would be, I think. May I bring her in?"

I put away my sermon notes and stood up, waiting.

The girl who hesitated in the doorway was more than unattractive. Unkempt hair and clothes and shoes, wrinkled stockings with crooked seams, an inch of slip showing —this was the least of it. Her face was pathetic. Upper front teeth distorted her lip and her right cheek; never had I seen another human so in need of orthodontics. Into my mind, like pellets fired in anger, came an awareness: *teeth.* TEETH. TEETH.

"This is Miss Lucy Emmett, Dr. Hornaday," Georgia said and hurriedly left the room. Once again she pointedly closed the door.

I moved up a chair for Miss Lucy Emmett and went back to my own behind the desk.

"What can I do for you, Miss Emmett?"

"I heard you on the radio last night," she said, sullenly. There was an awkward movement of her upper lip which on any other face would have been a wry smile. "When you said, *'Are you full of self-pity tonight?'* I was driving out to Padadena to the Arroyo Seco Bridge. You know what they've done out there?"

"Fixed it so nobody can jump off."

"The barbed wire goes way up and curves inward."

"That's right. There hasn't been a suicide off the bridge in years. You didn't know that?"

"I found it out!"—grimly.

A drive to Pasadena was not as messy as a slight slash across the wrists; less dangerous than not quite enough sleeping pills; invited less notoriety than the gas turned on with one window slightly open; the freeway wasn't crowded at midnight and a desperate, ugly girl could drive seventeen lonely miles embracing her misery, telling herself, for whatever negative satisfaction there was in it, that she wanted to die.

"I always have the radio on, without listening, but then I heard you asking those questions. When you said there wasn't a problem that couldn't be solved, I wondered how you'd go about getting me a date?"

She fixed her eyes on me with contempt; then she allowed her lip to fold back in what should have been a smile; she knew how shockingly grotesque she was. She had done this times without number into the mirror, I was sure. She was Hyde with no Jekyll to go back to. She knew I would have to look away, and I did. She had won a small, bleak victory.

"A date," I said. "Is that all you want?"

"It'd be a start," she taunted. "I've never had one. I'm twenty-seven years old." She added glumly: "I danced with a little fat boy once at an eighth-grade dance. We hated each other."

"However, you haven't really wanted a date lately," I told her.

"What makes you think so?"

"Your clothes. Your hair. Your nails. Those flats you're wearing. A girl who wants a date puts her best foot forward."

"My best foot forward couldn't possibly get ahead of my teeth," she said savagely. "That's all people see when they look at me. That's all *you* saw. When I stood in the doorway and you first saw me, I could read your mind. You thought: *Good heavens!* Or maybe you thought *Good God!* I've heard people whisper it when they first saw me: *Good God!*"

"As you may have gathered from the radio program, I happen to believe in a Good God," I said.

"That's where we differ. He sure wasn't around when *I* was born!"

So here was another one who was "mad at God."

Why hadn't someone taken her to an orthodontist when she was little? Why hadn't she gone herself when she grew up? She was sitting tensely with folded hands locked between her knees, eyes smoldering. I decided on a tiptoe approach.

"Do you ever attend church?"

A dry little chuckle was answer enough.

"Your family. They were religious?"

"Religious? They were religious fanatics! They didn't

believe in tampering with God's creation. They said God made me this way for reasons of His own."

"And you believed them?"

"Certainly. For a very long time, even through college. Nights I would lie close to my window and look up at the stars and ask God what I'd done to deserve this, and how I could make amends. There wasn't a night I didn't ask for His help. The sky is empty, Dr. Hornaday. The heavens are for stars and astronauts."

The questions I might have asked were in my mind, but I hesitated. And while I was hesitating, she grudgingly told me about her family. They lived in Whittier. She saw them rarely. She embarrassed them. Now she lived by herself in a kitchenette apartment off Wilshire and worked in the trust department of a Los Angeles bank. She had no friends.

"They keep me hidden in a back room at the bank," she said tartly. "But I'm efficient. I'm good at figures and I can spell and I know more about grammar than my employers."

She had done well in school. An eighth grade teacher, Mrs. Goodrich, had taken an interest in her, and fired her with the desire to excel. She would obviously have plenty of time to study. One Friday night Mrs. Goodrich, with her husband, had chaperoned an eighth-grade dance; it was she who had produced the fat boy. He wasn't popular either. They had done an unforgettable shuffle around the dance floor with everybody staring.

"The kids used to call me the Witch," Miss Emmett said. "But I got higher scores than any of them in college. I majored in government, history and economics and graduated Phi Beta Kappa from Cal."

"Where's your key?"

"I never wear it."

"Start wearing it," I said. "You'll begin the healing with that. If the negative side takes you to the Arroyo Seco Bridge, how about trying the affirmative?"

Suddenly she buried her face in her hands.

"I'm such a mess," she sobbed. "Oh, Dr. Hornaday, I wouldn't even know where to begin."

Her fingers were long and her hands were shapely; I complimented her and said she could begin by not biting her nails. She looked at me through tears. And now that I wasn't thinking about her teeth, I noticed that her blue eyes were placed wide apart and were lovely.

"You have a complexion many women would envy, beautiful eyes, a good figure, and youth," I said. "You have the credentials that go with scholarship, a good job and independence. You've a charming voice, resonant and agreeable, even under stress. For what perverse reason would you embrace a negative idea with such intensity that it has taken me until now to begin to see you as you really are? You're an intelligent young woman, and if you care to, you can be a very attractive one."

"Will you say that again, please?"

"I can tell you something that I know for sure, Miss Emmett. Your negative idea of yourself demands negative attention. What we really feel about ourselves, we become. You believe you're unattractive, lost to love, lost to happiness—your every word and action reveal it—and because you believe this, others believe it about you. But there is a Power within you which accepts responsibility for every problem when we seek a response from Life Itself and decide on a definite line of action."

That was as close as I dared go to suggesting a medical

solution. At some time in her years of independence she must have visited a dentist; or if she hadn't then there was a psychological imbalance here: she was punishing someone else, too, with her ugliness and her misery. But it was true, now that we had both stopped thinking *teeth,* I could become aware of her many good features.

"If you can realize that the only problem we have is with ourselves," I said, "you will then skip over nonessentials that have bothered you. We are not laboring with a God that is unwilling or a Power that is reluctant. Your desire rightly channeled is all the motivation you need.

"Now, before we have prayer together, I'd like to give you a thought or two to work on. Our prayer can be helpful only if it leads to an affirmative conviction that your life is on the upgrade. Prayer in itself does not heal. It is a process that leads to the conviction that heals. You had a conviction that you're ugly. I want you to have a conviction of beauty."

"But I *am* ugly."

"See what I mean?" I chided her. "This is not the way we pray. We must think in terms of the answer, not the problem. In the beginning it might be difficult to affirm, 'I am beautiful,' but the Spirit within you is beautiful and if you'll be vigilant with the affirmation concerning beauty, love, happiness, the Power within will not fail you. It knows what to do and when. You can count on It."

"You really believe that?" she asked, sitting up straighter.

"I really do. I know it's true. Now, let's pray." I said: "Infinite Presence, called on or not, we know that Thou art always present, that every prayer sincerely believed in is instantly acted upon. Through the Oneness of Thy Spirit of wisdom, love and truth, we speak the word of right action for Lucy Emmett. . . ."

After our prayer I gave her a paperback—*What Religious Science Teaches*—by Ernest Holmes and read her the paragraph which heads this chapter. She put the slim volume in her bag. Then she suddenly rummaged around and located a pair of gloves. She put them on and brushed at her skirt.

"I'd like to see you here again sometime," I said.

"When?"

"You'll know when."

She hesitated at the door.

"Thank you for the compliments," she said. "I truly don't think I ever had a compliment before."

On the way out she asked Georgia for the name of a good hairdresser. Then she lingered while they discussed the relative merits of Saks, Magnin's, Robinson's and Ohrbach's.

Georgia popped in as soon as the girl had gone.

"What's she going to *do?*"

"I believe she's going to use the Power within," I said.

It was a busy season with Easter coming, and the agenda for the seminar to be worked out; the whole staff forgot about the ugly girl. When I had said, "You'll know when to come back," I must have assumed that she would eventually find an oral surgeon and come back someday with gleaming dentures. But that wasn't the way it happened.

One Saturday morning Georgia phoned me at home. This was about six months after Lucy Emmett had been in the office, and the name didn't mean anything for a moment.

"Who?"

"Teeth!" Georgia said.

"Oh, my word, *yes*. Of course I remember."

"Well, she phoned, Dr. Bill. And I think she's still got the teeth. There's that little hiss on the *s*'s sometimes. But, anyhow, she wants to see you for a few minutes after eleven o'clock church tomorrow. She's got somebody she wants you to meet. I think it's a man."

"If it's a man, she's got dentures," I predicted. "Dentures sometimes produce a little hiss on the *s*'s."

But she didn't have dentures. I had come directly to my office after the second service and was hanging up my robe when Georgia came in. It was impossible to interpret her expression.

"Miss Lucy Emmett and Mr. Bruce Bourges are here, Dr. Hornaday."

Then she stepped aside and bowed them in.

Lucy came first, wearing a smart dark suit, hat, gloves and high-heeled suède pumps. The teeth weren't as noticeable—they didn't erase everything else in the room as they once had—but they were there, nothing had been done: but it was her eyes that held me. The melting look is one a minister recognizes from a distance—when a woman has put herself aside, utterly, because she is truly and wholeheartedly in love, there is an expression which can't be matched anywhere in nature, even in the spring. Lucy was in love. Lucy was deliriously happy.

The shock when I saw Bruce Bourges was of a reverse order and left me with a tumbling series of impressions. We shook hands and I tried to hide incredulity. He was a sensitive looking, extraordinarily handsome man in his early thirties. His suit was of excellent texture and tailor-made, his tie was tasteful, and he had a shy, attractive manner.

Con man, I thought. Instantly, I remembered that I hadn't learned how well-to-do Lucy's family might have been. The thought raced into my mind that her parents were wealthy, had passed away and left her a fortune.

The young man didn't waste any time. "I would like to see you alone for a moment, if I may, sir."

Lucy blushed. "Why can't we both tell him about us?" she asked, and then, all aglow, turned to me. "Bruce works at the bank, and I take his dictation, and everything you told me about—you know—the Power within—well, Bruce is interested, too—"

He gently broke in.

"Now, look, Luce," he said. "I told you I wanted to see him alone for a minute. You came here with your problems—now let me come with mine."

She flashed the ring on her engagement finger. It was a diamond; the glitter of the stone was all but reflected in her eyes.

"It happened two weeks ago," she told me, and squeezed his hand. "I'll go talk to Georgia."

After the door had closed, Bruce Bourges quickly said, "I know your time is valuable, and I'm embarrassed to ask you this favor, but I really love Lucy." He was very shy. "She's the most wonderful girl in the world." His voice quavered with honest emotion. "She's brilliant, you know—they think the world of her at the bank—she's loyal, and warmhearted and bright—a Phi Beta Kappa and all that. She's really remarkable. But there's one thing I can't bring up now, it's too personal. She's never had her teeth fixed because she couldn't afford it. She went to find out about it once and it was more than she could ever manage. For years now she's sent some of her pay check to her parents—

they've really had problems." He took out his wallet. "I know she'd be happier if her teeth were fixed, and she'd be beautiful, too. Just between us, Dr. Hornaday, I've also had obligations but I have four hundred dollars here and I'd like to make a down payment with it—do you know a good oral surgeon?"

I was nodding; stunned and nodding and ashamed. I wanted to apologize and couldn't. "Forgive me, Father," I said inside.

In a few moments we were chatting like old friends. Bruce Bourges' diffidence masked an inner strength. He had been brought up by a severe elderly aunt in a New England village; he'd never been at ease with girls. In college his social life had been anything but successful. After bumbling his way into a date, he'd often make a mess of it—often as not freeze, unable to talk. Even now, in his thirties, he'd taken a long time to speak to Lucy. From the beginning he had admired Lucy's efficiency and intelligence, and he liked her voice. So many western voices were flat and nasal. After dictating letters to her, he discovered that she knew as much about finance as any bank officer. He admired her very much. Then shortly after Easter she came in one Monday wearing a new summery outfit, with her hair combed in a charming way, and he figured if he didn't ask her for a date, somebody else would beat him to it. So he asked her to dinner. The pause was so long he was afraid she was going to decline, but she said, "Thank you—when?" After that they had no trouble talking. The night he gave her the engagement ring she told him why she was wearing the Phi Beta Kappa key, and how a visit to the church had changed her thinking. He saw his chance, then, to ask someone else to help him. He didn't want to embarrass her. He was sure she was sensitive about her teeth—but brave; you had to be a woman of character to override such a handicap.

"We'll call a conference of orthodontists," I told him happily. "One of them will surely want to write a paper about such a case. We'll handle this."

And so we did.

Radiant is a weary adjective reserved for society pages in small-town weeklies in June, but it must be dusted off here because on her wedding day Lucy Emmett's glow came from deep inside and never faded.

Not long ago, for this record, Lucy was asked if she could remember what she had done and *thought* after leaving the office the first time. (We are good friends now—I recently baptized their second child). She remembered most of it very clearly. Some of my remarks had stung. She'd hurried home, changed her clothes and plunged into housecleaning: sent slips to the laundry and skirts to the cleaner's, washed her hair, and then got into the tub to read. Ernest's little book was confusing at first. It was like discovering that the world was round after always having been told that it was flat. Working at it, trying to accept the proposition that this is a universe of Love and Law, was an improvement on wallowing in misery.

In the days that followed, whenever she started to slide back into that "dark, delicious despair," she checked herself. The dark, delicious despair—Lucy's phrase—had been a perverse way of punishing her parents for their early neglect of her desperate need—except that it didn't punish them but hurt only herself. She said:

"I'd had insomnia, so each night, instead of counting sheep I'd work on affirmative ideas first. I remembered the compliments, so I would say, over and over, '*I have beauti-*

ful eyes, a good figure, a charming voice, and I am bright and have a Phi Beta key to prove it. I'm going to wear the key with new sweaters and new skirts and sheer stockings. I shall have my teeth fixed as soon as I can afford to and I'll start saving *now.*'

"Next, I would love, bless and forgive my family. Then I worked out a formula which I would repeat until I had fallen asleep. I'd say: 'My body is a manifestation of the Living Spirit. It is created and sustained by one Presence and one Power.' Then I would *think* about what that meant. Sometimes I would wake up in the morning with a deeper understanding of it. And incidentally, I attended your church service each Sunday—sat in the last row of the balcony. That helped, too.

"Then one lovely day I went to work with a light heart in a gay new sweater and skirt, and I *knew* that from the back I was as attractive as anybody. Then I thought I could be attractive in front, too, if I were friendly and easy with people, so I tried that.

"Bruce noticed me. He had been kind even in my worst period, but now he noticed me a lot. He was shy, though. Several days before he got up nerve to ask for a date, I knew what was in his mind. Then at night before I went to sleep I *knew* he would ask me. I would go to sleep *knowing* it—and I really *did* know it, too; it wasn't just hope. I can't imagine what his aunt did to him, but she left him scared of girls. He needed somebody who admired him and wanted to listen to him, and I told myself I was the perfect one to listen and to make him happy. The funny thing is that he admired me, too. He likes excellence in work, and dedication, and loyalty. When he did ask me, I was afraid for a minute I'd never collect my wits to say 'Yes,' but I did.

"That first date I told him that when I could afford it I was going to have my teeth fixed; then I never mentioned them again. Sometimes I actually didn't think about my teeth for days. That was certainly a change.

"Isn't it strange? This is the same world I was in the night I drove to the Arroyo Seco Bridge. But I would never recognize it; it's beautiful now."

What changed it was a prayer of affirmation which came from her heart; she filled her universe with it night and day.

"I certainly learned a lesson," she told me gratefully.

And so did I.

The learning was continuous and the change in my own life almost incredible. It was a period when many people were seeking new dimensions and within a few weeks our Sunday service at the Belmont was forced to move to a larger theater, the Uptown, and then into a still larger one, the Wiltern with its twenty-three hundred seats; and when we outgrew that I urged Ernest to build a church, a Founder's Church which would meet all our requirements. Hundreds of others were urging this, and offering to help, and it might have gone smoothly enough except that the Founder himself stood adamantly in the way, content to post the Standing Room Only sign at both theaters—and thus a six year struggle began.

8

Double Negatives Reversed

"The irresistible force meets the immovable object," Ernest said amiably. "Let's go for a walk, Bill."

It was the Monday after Easter. Scores of people had been turned away from both theaters the day before. And from both services. New arguments for a church of our own had brought me into town early and Ernest had found me pacing outside his office. He had listened, as always, serene, adamant, a majority of one. And said No.

But I persisted. There had been confusion in three places. More children than we could hope to accommodate had turned up for Sunday school at the Institute. Many of our regulars, after driving miles to the Wiltern or the Beverly, had been turned away—whereupon they'd come back in all their finery to cool their heels in the parking lot until the Sunday school classes were dismissed. I'd emphasized the argument with a fist hammering on the desk.

"Let's walk over to the park," he said, and led the way.

But he stopped abruptly in the foyer. Peter Ganine, the sculptor, had made a bronze bust of Ernest. Hazel had insisted on placing it near the entrance. And here it was, a work of art which will survive any normal weather: it captures the philosopher for posterity, the shape of his head, his intact attitude, a hint of his humor.

"Ernest," he said over his shoulder as we went by, "the student thinks he can play the banjo better'n him that taught him."

His words reached me with a sharp sting. We walked in silence toward the playground on Fourth Street. The City of Angels was at its sparkling best that morning. A three-day wind from the Mojave had blown itself out on Saturday and now the sky was clean except for a white vapor trail streaking westward into the blue.

"We don't need a church, Bill," he said calmly, picking up the argument as we walked. "This is a *teaching* ministry, remember. The Institute is adequate—always has been." He added, "Except, of course, on special days. We've plenty of room for meditation meetings. Plenty of classrooms. Y'see, a big sanctuary would be used on Sunday —empty during the week. That's wasteful. Sorry to be obstinate but the answer is an affirmative *No*. We're doing fine. We'll preserve what we have."

He covered familiar territory: he himself had lectured happily in hotel ballrooms—the Biltmore Bowl, the Ambassador—and the larger theaters all his professional life. The rented places were comfortable, adequately heated and air-conditioned. They offered no maintenance problem. No insurance problem. No staff, no janitors. Pay a rental fee and that was the end of it. You delivered a Sunday lecture and went home—free to write, meditate, study. Problems of organization didn't interrupt the quiet hours that were important to men doing creative work. Where was the argument? Everything was perfect.

"But the pressure's building up—that's the argument," I said. "More and more people are talking about having a church of our own. They want it very much."

"Can you be sure? This could be the natural reaction to an inconvenience on an occasional Sunday. Ask yourself this question, Bill: Why do they come to hear us, jam-packed to the galleries, looking gay and relaxed on Sunday? Could it be because it's *not* a church? Many reverent people want to escape ecclesiasticism—that's what frustrated their religious impulse when they were young! Ask 'em—they'll tell you so. As a matter of fact, yesterday was too churchy to suit me. Oh, well," he added honestly, "I'll have to admit the congregation liked the flowers."

"Certainly they liked the flowers. And that's what they long for—your kind of thinking in a church of their own."

My own service at the Wiltern long had been presented in a flowery setting on Easter morning, and yesterday Ernest had been persuaded to dress up the Beverly stage with ferns and Easter lilies. He'd gone that far—but I had gone farther. The congregation at the Wiltern had been asked to arrive early and bring potted Easter lilies which could be arranged on the stage and taken home after the service. The response had been enormous. But many people had been delayed in the heavy traffic and passers-by on Wilshire watched with amusement the not-even-standing-room crowds milling around under the marquee with their potted plants. Our ushers and the victims failed to find the humor in it.

I touched this item like a home-run hitter rounding second base and then plunged on:

"When we build our—" this debate called for semantics—"our *edifice,* the sanctuary will not be empty during the week. Noon meditation meetings will attract hundreds of people from the Wilshire district. The chapel can be open all day. And what about weddings? The young people want a wedding chapel. And teen-agers—dozens of 'em—have asked for regular evening study groups. We need room for AA meetings, art classes, coffee klatsches. But most of all, the Sunday school's the problem, Ernest, and it's not just on Easter. We're bursting at the seams. We've got to expand or give up. So let's build an adequate . . . edifice, an attractive modern structure without marquees."

"What's wrong with marquees?"

I could tell him. The Wiltern marquee had greeted our congregation one Sunday with huge illumined letters: TO HELL AND BACK. Audie Murphy, starring in the screen version of his book, had been drawing large crowds matinee and evening; but on a quiet Sunday morning the irreverent words seemed to come into the theater with the congregation. People were unusually subdued and thoughtful, reminded perhaps, as I was, that some of the upcoming screen titles were even less fitting; and then, always, there were lobby displays: bare shoulders, bosoms, toothy monsters, terrified girls, and guns. Bang bang.

I mentioned this, too—possibly hit it a little hard. But Ernest was merely amused. Then I bore down.

He was always pleased when his ministers built their own churches. It was happening all over America. Some of our people had created buildings which dramatized light—churches with glass walls on either side, with the pews set down in gardens. Ernest often attended dedication services and was at his best when he spoke to the first congregation in churches founded on the Truth of the Universality of the Christ Spirit.

"That's all well and good," he said when I quoted from an address he'd given in a nearby town a few days before. "Those churches are an inevitable development. But I want the Institute to serve as a teaching ministry, and that's all. That was the original idea, and it's practical."

"Now, look, Dr. Holmes, someday, whether you like it or not, a church will be erected in your memory." That alarmed him. "You've founded a religious movement—it's reasonable, and it works. Somebody is sure to build a monument to you. If you fight it while you're here, they'll do it when you're gone."

"Oh, no, no, no." It was a moan.

"It's inevitable. The building should be designed to reflect the philosophy. Who is better qualified to decide on the style? If *you* help with it, we can avoid pots of burning incense, graven images. Why, suppose somebody wound up worshiping that bronze bust of you by Peter Ganine—"

"They wouldn't dare!"

"You know how things go sometimes. The way to avoid it is to build an edifice now."

Another item had been saved for the softening-up process. He was still talking but I threw it in:

"After the service yesterday a man offered us ten thousand dollars' worth of blue chip stock if we'll buy the property next door, get an architect, and start planning an—"

"Edifice—" he snapped and left me.

I watched him dodge traffic. He went up the wide steps

into the playground and found a park bench. When I joined him, he was sitting with hands on knees, shoulders hunched, deep in thought.

He reached for a loafer and took it off. When he was irritated, he often discovered pebbles and shook them out wherever he happened to be. Such roomy shoes perhaps invited pebbles, though he only seemed to mind them when he was otherwise disturbed. I pressed on at the risk of his disfavor; there'd never be a better time.

"You've evolved something new, Ernest. And it's got to have a place to grow comfortably," I argued. "Remember what Emerson said: 'America shall introduce a pure religion.' "

"I have evolved a philosophy," Ernest countered a bit sharply. "I can give you something else Emerson said. Now listen to this"—and he quoted without pausing for word or phrase—his great gift, that incredible memory:

" 'There will be a new church founded on moral science; at first cold and naked, a babe in the manger again, the algebra and mathematics of ethical law, the church of men to come, without shawms or psaltery or sackbut; but it will have heaven and earth for its beams and rafters; science for symbol and illustration; it will fast enough gather beauty, music, picture, poetry. It shall send man home to his central solitude and make him know that much of the time he must have himself for his friend. He shall expect no co-operation, he shall walk with no companion. The nameless Thought, the nameless Power, the super-personal Heart—he shall repose alone on that. He needs only his own verdict. No good fame can help, no bad fame can hurt him. The Laws are his consolers, the good Laws themselves are alive, they know if he keep them, they animate him with the leading of great duty, and an endless horizon.' "

He studied me triumphantly. "I like best the part where he says, 'the church will have heaven and earth for its beams and rafters.' Emerson saw the new church in man's own heart and under the stars."

He was content. He thought he'd stopped me.

"Then why are we teaching?"

I had asked it hotly. He was startled not by my question but by the emotion. Once upon a time I had been on a debating team at Whittier College, with a certain Richard M. Nixon, and in our youth and enthusiasm we hadn't tried to avoid heat.

"Pardon?" he said.

"Why don't we step aside and allow each man to find the philosophy for himself, the way you did, then, Ernest? Billions of people are on the earth. We reach only a handful. Why do we bother at all?"

He hunched his shoulders again.

"Scholars with a sense of obligation to students who would follow them made their teaching available for me," he said. "Their discoveries were in the libraries when I began my search. I've gone to much labor to bring this philosophy together; I'll save the next generation a little time." His voice dwindled away, but he added: "And you know why we're teaching in theaters—because more people want to hear about this than we could crowd into the lecture halls."

"Right—so many want to hear it first hand that we can't accommodate them in two theaters and the Institute. You like the idea of the Sunday school. You *want* youngsters to grow up in faith, without fear—I've heard you say it. And there's more compassion in your philosophy than I find in metaphysics generally. You're a sentimental man. A warm heart presents the equations and formulae. Now I've got to hit you hard. Forgive me, but I think a childhood prejudice has kept you from reaching a logical conclusion."

He was flushed.

"I have no childhood prejudice."

"What about the baptism?"

"What baptism?"

"Yours."

"Who told you about that?"

"You did. Twice."

"Twice! Stop me when I tell 'em twice!"

I'd heard it times without number, as a matter of fact. The anecdote long ago had become part of his teaching. There are people who still claim that Ernest Holmes had been a Christian Scientist; this is untrue. Once, in his searching, he had taken private lessons from Clara Showers, a reader in the Mother Church at Boston, but he had rejected certain basic tenets in the philosophy of the remarkable and greatly gifted Mrs. Eddy. When her followers talked about mental malpractice, he objected—such did not exist except as one *accepted* malpractice—and he had been alarmed by the exclusiveness of organization and the rigid forms into which the publications had fallen. His study sent him back to the sources—Emerson, Quimby, Troward, Plotinus, Pico della Mirandola, William James and others. He told his audiences that he had been a Baptist. Indeed, it had been his own baptism, in boyhood, which had shaken him, thus preparing him for Emerson and the happy day when the seer's essay on Self-Reliance raised him from a sickbed to send him on a lifetime exploration of the Power within.

He had been one of nine brothers. He was born on January 21, 1887, in Lincoln, Maine. His mother at sixteen had been a schoolteacher, his father a self-educated farmer; the startling ideas of the New England transcendentalists often were debated in the household; but even so he had been baptized in the conventional fashion—immersion.

One Sunday he found himself soaking wet with the word "salvation" still ringing in his ears.

He had been a chubby, inquiring boy, always with an embarrassing question on the tip of his tongue. That Sunday he cornered the minister on the steps.

"Reverend, tell me on your honor, now—" he pointed a finger, "do you really think baptism is necessary to salvation?"

The good man glanced over his shoulder.

"Son," he said, nervously, lowering his voice, "I don't actually know—but why take a chance?"

It was here, when Ernest told the story publicly, that he paused and with an actor's perfect timing added:

"That's when I first looked into Buddhism."

And now I had countered too hard.

"I have no prejudice against any religion, Bill," he said, gravely. "I reserve the right to ask questions—like the one I asked our minister when I was a boy—but religious people who can accommodate enlarging concepts within the ancient forms—and many do—are all turning to the same God, and finding answers in the same Mind. I have never told that story in prejudice, or held any prejudice. And I've always respected the minister for his honesty. He himself was comfortable in his doubts. Nothing prodded him into going deeper. This wasn't true of me."

I persisted. "And now the crowds gather because you have evolved a philosophy which you yearn to share. And here in the twentieth century, in the heart of an industrial complex, even Emerson might agree that people of like mind—and their children—should reasonably expect to meet in comfort for the study of this Truth."

Ernest was up and walking. I followed. We strode back to the Institute in silence. Then he sat down on the steps in his favorite spot, near the west pillar, and when I caught up, he gave me a sweet, forgiving smile and indicated the top step. He'd never been angry at me, though he'd come close today; but now he had forgiven me and soon made it clear that in his opinion the church debate had been closed for good. He was ready to play the label game to divert our minds and bring us back to laughter.

A young man trudged by with lips puckered as if he had just tasted a quince.

"Label?" Ernest asked.

"Missed it."

"It was in an invisible four-inch bamboo frame on his chest. He's an Injustice Collector. That's a dandy hobby. He's holding onto antiques to see what he can get for them."

"What do you think he'll get?"

"Mumps," he said. "Possibly arthritis. Backaches."

I decided not to let him get away with this.

"Ernest, I'm not going to give up on this church idea. I suppose I should warn you—I'm treating on it."

It seemed to me our glances held much too long to be friendly, but at last the pixie humor flashed in his eyes.

"I understand you're starting a Symptom-a-day club," he said.

I sighed. "It was just an idea. I used it in a sermon."

"How do you work it?"

Losing out again but retreating in good order, I said:

"It's for people who put a claim on symptoms. They wake up in the morning and before they're out of bed, they make a quick check for something to complain about. They cry—oh, my back. Or: oh, my ulcer. Or: my nerves. Or: my head. And they hurry out to breakfast, looking as miserable as possible, to announce the negative symptom for the day. They embrace it—"mine, all mine, and I love it." Anybody can join the Symptom-a-day club. No dues. No officers. No meetings. No restrictions on race or creed. Anybody can get in and suffer."

"Sounds pretty democratic all right."

"Oh, it's wide open. It's so democratic we've lately taken in aristocrats with hay fever. A penny a symptom and we'd have a million dollars for a church in no time."

This wasn't fair. He had changed the subject. He said severely:

"Psychosomatic illness can seem very real, Bill." His face assumed the solemnity which accompanied his better jokes. "You've heard the one about the hypochondriac who finally shuffled off? Carved in two-inch letters on his tombstone was the taunt: *Now will you believe I was sick?*"

Last time he told it there had been an explosion of laughter. My response was a disappointment. But, anyway, the point had been blurred by the burn of rubber on the pavement; a Yellow Cab ran the red light on the corner, stopped twenty yards beyond us with a squeal of brakes and now was backing up. A saturnine driver, unshaved, middle-aged, wearing a soiled leather jacket, and with a shabby regulation cap cocked belligerently on his head, parked at the curb opposite us. He glanced at a slip of paper, shut off his motor and tramped up the steps muttering: "Crackpot dame!"

"Label?" Ernest asked.

"I thought it said *trapped.*"

Ernest chuckled. "From where I'm sitting it said *damned.*"

A moment later my secretary appeared beside us. She looked flustered.

"There's a cab driver with a note for you, Dr. Bill." She handed it to me. "He says he's promised to let you talk to him for five minutes."

The note was from one of the professional practitioners. It said:

> Dear Dr. Bill:
>
> This will introduce Julius Podholz, the most alarming case of negative thinking I've ever encountered. He is like an accident going somewhere to happen. I simply couldn't get through to him, but now he has agreed to spend five minutes talking with you. Do what you can. He needs help.
>
> Marian

Ernest accepted the note, read it and handed it back.

"You see? You don't need a church to help Julius." He added crisply and got up, "Let me know how it turns out."

There was the impasse, brick on brick. We would henceforth walk around it.

The cadence and quality of true Brooklyn speech is impossible to reproduce on paper. It is more than sound and accent; in its highest expression most words carry a chip on the shoulder, and grammar is used as a club.

"Dis crazy dame gimme five bucks to listen to you five minutes, doc," Julius Podholz said when I met him in the hall outside my office. "Start talkin'." He glanced at his watch.

I went in, but he lingered in the hall. Ernest's honorary degrees, twenty-seven of them (which he refused to hang in his own office or any other conspicuous place), were in the dark little passageway.

"Hey—you a head shrinker?" Julius asked.

I explained briefly as he came in. There were two comfortable chairs, but he selected a straight one and sat on the edge of it. I had now graduated from the Fish Bowl into Hazel Holmes' former office. She had given it to me when she retired.

"When did you leave Brooklyn?" I asked.

"Smart Joe, notice my accent, huh? I left one whole terrible year ago, doc. I was outa m'mind. Outa the fryin' pan into the fire, that's me. Any dimwit woulda known. Not Podholz."

"Things aren't going well?"

"Things stink, doc."

"How did you happen to come west?"

"Sunshine. Ha, ha. Sarah, m'wife, talks up California sunshine. Ha, ha. You ever see the sun t'rough the smog, doc? Right away I get asthma, can't smoke, gain eighteen pounds, headaches and feel sick. But the kids get big California appetites, eat like monsters. You know how many meals I gotta provide? Eighteen a day. In a week it's eighty-nine. In a month it's two hunnerd seventy-two. In a year it's asternomical. And me gettin' nickel tips. Bro-*ther!* Ah, for the noise and stink and freezin' cold and sweatin' heat o' Brooklyn! But I'm stuck now."

Trapped. Surrounded. Damned. We were right.

"Know what was back of it?" he went on, hitching his chair closer. "Sarah fingered it out—" he put a forefinger in the middle of his forehead. "She fingered she'd pry me outa them Saturday crap games the first day I win, if I ever did—and I did. Onct. By accident. California sunshine, she says, and out we come, those chompin' monsters eatin' hamburgers like locusts across all them states and deserts. Lookin' for sunshine, see?—and landed in the thick black smog. It's par. That's me. That's Podholz."

"How old are you, Julius?"

"Younger'n I look, doc. I aged lately. Nothin' ages a hacker like a nickel tip."

"How do you earn a nickel tip?"

"You got the right word, doc. I sure earned it. You know what I done? I carried grocery sacks up three flights of rickety stairs for a little old lady. And she gimme five cents —in pennies yet. That's the bottom of a long, lousy, downhill slide." He shot a soiled cuff and looked at his watch again. "Start yakkin', doc. I'm holdin' still for it. Five bucks for five minutes the lady gimme—first big tip in the Golden State. Hey. What kinda racket *is* this, anyhow?"

"At the moment I'm doing research for a book," I explained. It was an inspiration. "Tell me, have you got a good cab?"

"Me? A good cab?" He poked his chest repeatedly with a stiff thumb. "Doc, you never saw anybody get so many lemons. I get lemons alla*time*. I had a tire blow out when I wasn't even sittin' in it. I'm on a stool havin' coffee. Another time I'm parked at a hashhouse, see, havin' a lunch, an' guess what? A juven-ile skids around the corner and bashes m'fender flat. How's that for terrible? Once, on a freeway at night, my gas tank sprung a leak for no reason, but I didn't find it out until we was in the *country*—and my fare was a fat, gimpy guy with a sprained ankle late for his appointment, and I hadta almost carry him a mile. And *that* brought on rain. He had a big bleedin' heart like everybody out here. He tips me two bits and then digs around and adds another nickel. Thirty cents. Big deal."

"Tell me more about Sarah."

"Sarah? She's got a *thing,* doc. She's tryin' for culture, see? Like yestiddy. In a bus she finds this magazine somebody threw away. Gourmey—it's spelled with a *t* but you say it *Gourmey.* This is hot stuff. Me gettin' nickel tips, so now she wants to cook with butter and serve or-dourvey. Imagine them monsters eatin' or-dourvey?"

"Life's been using you pretty hard, has it?"

His cap had been spinning on his finger. He let it run down.

"Now, look, doc," he said suspiciously. "Life don't use me no harder'n anybody else. Life stinks. It's hell."

"How does Sarah feel about it?"

"Huh? How should she feel? She's one of them dolls that keep chokin' back the tears. I like it better when they bust right out and cry."

"Do you love her?"

He stared at me. I asked:

"Does she love you?"

"Huh?"

"Did you love each other when you were married?"

"Hey, what *is* this racket? This one of them marriage consultations—"

Something prompted me to say:

"How would you like to make another five dollars?"

The words surprised us both. I'll never know why I said it. He gave me steely attention. Then he put his cap on, reached back with a stiff forefinger and pushed it down to the bridge of his nose, tilted his head to look at me with his eyes shadowed by the visor. The gesture conveyed caution, contempt and his imminent departure.

"Doin' what, doc?"

"Research."

"Yeah? This gonna be a paper chase? Where next?"

"I want you to try an experiment, Julius—whether it works or not, I'll give you five dollars at this time Friday morning."

"Yeah? Experiment with what?"

"Your attitude of mind."

His lips moved. He was repeating my words to himself. They'd conveyed no meaning.

"This is the Institute of Religious Science," I explained carefully. "We have a theory which has proved out consistently for almost forty years. We believe that every man, including Julius Podholz, has within him something which can be used to change everything he dislikes in his own life."

He hitched up his pants, cocked his head and regarded me sidewise. But he was listening.

"There's a technique," I went on. "Everything in life responds to our attitudes, our ideas. If you think people are unappreciative, they will be. If you expect a bad day—you'll have one. If your mind is grudgingly fixed on small tips—small tips you'll get. Or none. If your service is rendered only for money—you may miss out entirely. Now, then. Your present attitude has brought you nickel tips. You admit it. It has also given you a shabby cap, a soiled jacket, five o'clock shadow, hard luck and cabs that break down. If I show you the technique—tell you exactly how to do this—will you reverse your attitude, sweat out the affirmative, and report to me on Friday?"

Again he repeated words as if they held no meaning.

"*Reverse* my attitude?"

"Flip it over. You view everything through the glass darkly. Are you so stubborn you'd insist that's the only aspect there is?"

"Sweat out the affirmative—" he said, repeating.

"It won't be easy. You'll *earn* your five dollars—if you manage to be consistent between now and Friday. You'll have to climb out of the hell you say you're in."

"Yeah?"

"A self-created hell, the only kind there is. Are you capable of discipline?" He had shifted his weight to one leg and now stood with his hands in his hip pockets, head back, as if ideas had reached him with such impact as to rock him to one side. "You'll have to watch every thought, every word you say, and you'll substitute love for hate. Willing to try it? Or do you think you're too far gone?"

He stiffened.

"What comes first, pal?" he asked harshly.

"First courtesy, which is one aspect of love you may not have tried lately. When a fare hails you, greet him cheerfully. Get out and open the door."

He was stunned. "Get out and open the—"

"Exactly. And smile—if you think you can crack that frozen face of yours. Allow no negative remarks past your lips. Nobody sees the whole truth, Julius—there are as many viewpoints as there are people, but you have a choice and until Friday you're to take the bright side."

He was mildly interested. "It's kind of a gimmick, huh?"

"It's like the switch on a TV set. Try it. You might possibly tune in."

"So? Then what?"

"You'll succeed if you clarify your motives. Think it out first. Let's have a policy for the cab. Every successful business operates on a policy. It may help if you pretend that *you* are taking the cab. No matter what the provocation, treat the customer as you'd want to be treated."

His face darkened with recognition. One hand swept scornfully downward.

"A-h-h-h. *That* old hogwash. Don't kid me, doc. I went to Temple a few times. 'What hurts you, don't do to the other guy.' That's nothin' but the old-time Jewish *religion* —they talk that same junk to the kids. That's old stuff, goes way back."

"Ever tried it?"

"It ain't practical in the cab business."

"I think it is. That's my point. Five dollars for a good, hard try. Anybody made you any better offer?"

He rocked from heel to toe.

"You got a little bitty office for such a cheerful guy with such big ideas," he taunted.

"One day you'll find me in a bigger one with a glass wall and a garden outside."

"Yeah?"

"At the moment it's an idea—but that's where everything starts. My idea will become concrete block and glass eventually—with the help of a few thousand other people who also hold the vision of a beautiful new church."

"Yeah?"

"Listen, Julius. If it goes no further than this, understand this much: you have yourself for a friend—*that* you know for sure. What kind of friend are you being to yourself when every thought in your mind is destructive?"

He abruptly turned his back on me and walked into the hall. But his footsteps slowed and he returned to the doorway. For a moment he stood staring at me. Then with a smile that wasn't quite a grimace he swept a low, sardonic bow.

"Wanna ride with Smiley Podholz, pal?" he asked.

It was unintentionally very funny and I roared with laughter. A comedian lurks in the soul of all true Brooklynites; it had been a long time since Julius had got such a laugh. A slow grin showed big, even teeth; a long dormant humor stirred within him. His salute placed him as a onetime GI. He went out chuckling.

And that was that.

The phone rang. Sermons to write, broadcasts to outline, people to see. I forgot about Julius Podholz until later in the afternoon, when driving Ernest to the airport—he was lecturing in San Francisco that evening. I told him about the interview and brought him up to date.

"The man's in for a tremendous surprise if he'll be consistent," Ernest said. "Let's treat for him." He closed his eyes. "Julius Podholz will discover the warmth, the love within him; and in his every encounter people will respond. Julius will awaken to the Truth that there is one Source of all Supply. God, through him, is in action now. And so it is."

These days I was often aware of Ernest's loneliness; it was in the quality of the silence into which he dropped without warning, in his attitude toward his co-workers and in his effort to manifest the same lively interest in the world around him. A year before, Hazel had gone without warning, with ease, without pain; but the big house echoed without her, there were too many empty rooms; too much time on his hands; too little laughter. He had begun an ambitious project in verse in collaboration with his brother, Dr. Fenwicke Holmes. He welcomed the difficulties and before long opened the channels and worked with mounting excitement. Lena the housekeeper had told me that of late he often worked the whole night through. This epic poem later was published as *The Voice Celestial.*

He had asked me to conduct Hazel's funeral; and lonely as he was from the moment of her going, his belief in survival had been unshaken; the chapter on Immortality in his classic *Science of Mind* would stand as written. He had said: "Our bodies are like a river, forever flowing. The Indwelling Spirit alone maintains identity." He would see her again. He would join her. He had his work to finish, and then . . .

An unspoken thought reached me as we drove across town. Younger people would carry on. Had something I said in our debate brought about a change in attitude since morning? The atmosphere was more relaxed. That afternoon on the drive he was no doubt rehearsing for the San Francisco lecture, trying out on me his own unique clarification of the difference between the psychics and the mystics. Over a period of years, he had investigated psychic phenomena; with his usual scholarly thoroughness he had made it a point to meet and know many of the leading investigators and mediums of the day.

Later he summed up his findings in one of the Seminar

Lectures—available still in a small book of the same name edited by Georgia C. Maxwell. He made this comparison: send the psychics over the mountain range, he said, and ask them to return and report on their findings, and each would tell a different story. But not so the mystics. Separated by centuries, by cultures, by religions, each returns with the same report.

"When we put all the stories together," he said, "we find that except for the difference in language, the mystics all see the same thing and hear the same thing. Wouldn't we say, then, that they've been to the same place?

"This is the difference between them. . . . Intuition is the direct perception of Truth without any of the intellectual manipulation. It is to the *spiritually illumined* that we must turn for such knowledge of the Kingdom of God as we may acquire to add to that which we all intuitively feel. Walt Whitman said: 'There is more to man than is contained between his head and his bootstraps.' We should read Whitman, Meister Eckhart, St. Augustine, St. Teresa, Rufus Jones, Evelyn Underhill, Rudyard Kipling, Wordsworth, Whittier and Robert Browning. Why? Because they are speaking the language not of the unknowable but of the unknown. They are the ones who bring the news of the Kingdom of God, not the theologians who have made up their minds that God damns everybody who doesn't agree with them. There is no damnation other than our own little individual 'hells' which cool off as we gain confidence in the God that is beyond all human concept, in the God that *is,* not the God that is often enough believed in. . . . Let us look to the illumined for Truth. If anyone knew it, Jesus knew it. 'Neither do I condemn thee; go and sin no more.'

He was projecting love but not deserting law. Great mystics have taught that every soul is on the pathway of an eternal evolution and will get 'there.' Browning said: 'I shall arrive as the birds assume their trackless path.' "

He was exercising his gift for detachment even as he spoke. It was in the timbre of his voice, in the quiet way he sat beside me, in the words he said. With something akin to alarm I thought: Ernest has known the world longer than most. His scholarship from boyhood on had taken him through eons of man's incredible behavior, into the dustiest manuscripts of the past, fearlessly through the cruelties and triumphs of our own twentieth century, and into the lofty findings of the most illumined—the men and women who had explored the ultimate shining glory in all ages, among all peoples. His faith in a universe of Law and Love had been steadfast in boyhood and was steadfast now. But he was desperately lonely.

As we waited for his plane at the gate, I sensed a new weariness.

"Bill, if you'll come over to lunch after the lecture Sunday," he said, wistfully, "I'll put together a New England menu. Your favorite beans, um? They're the ones Hazel liked, too." He added, as they announced his plane: "And I'll want to hear all about Julius Podholz."

The sturdy figure went through the gate. When he had crossed the shadowed asphalt runway and climbed the steps it occurred to me that in all the years I'd known him, he had never once looked back.

Friday morning I was writing a sermon in my office when a yellow cap sailed past me and landed on the floor near the desk. It was worn, battered, but somehow jaunty. Julius Podholz, grinning from ear to ear, came in to retrieve it. He held out a hard hand.

"Keep your five bucks, doc," he shouted. "Bro-ther! It sure *works!*"

"Things are all right now?"

"All *right!* Well, no. Everything but Sarah. Everything else is terrific."

"What's wrong with Sarah?"

He closed the door and came back.

"No communercation," he told me as if the word were new. This time he took a comfortable chair and sat down as if he owned it. "She's got it in her head I been shootin' craps, see?" He showed me a stuffed wallet. "Look, you know what I made for myself, take-home pay, since I seen you? One hunnerd and forty-six bucks. You need any dough, doc?"

We grinned at each other.

"What happened, Julius?"

"Miracles," he said. "For a while I think it's a—what'd you say?—coincidence. Then pretty soon it can't be, doc. It's impossible. It'll give you the chills. You know the first guy I got, when I left here? Listen: I cruise over to the Chapman Park Hotel, see, and there's a old guy waitin' and no cabs. He's a sad-faced, gray-haired, tired fella. I jumped out and open the door. He seems surprised! 'Why, *thank you,*' he says. He wants to go to the airport so I begin tellin' him how great the freeways are. This *reversed* what I allus said about 'em, see? Like you said? And the more I talk, the better they begin to look. More convenient-like, and faster. And then I think of all the trouble the engineers went to, mowing down houses, getting quit claims, alla legal stuff.

Man! I notice there's a kinda warm silence in the back seat, and when I look in the rear-view, this old guy smiles like somebody made love to him. You know what? It turns out he's on the highway commission, Sacramento, and he never heard no kind word about highways for fifteen-twenty years.

"He's got fifty-five minutes before his plane, and he says how about lunch—he wants the report from a hacker, see, outa the horse's mouth. So he don't care how I look, see, and he takes me to this swell airport joint for chow. I keep pumping up good ideas about the freeways—compliments, see, and I *feel* it—I get kinda drunk on it—and he takes notes in a little book. He follows me all the way to the door, we shake hands, and he gimme a twenty-dollar bill, fare plus about thirteen-fourteen-dollar tip. I begin to shake all over.

"I'm *stunned,* see? My cab is parked in the lot and I go reeling over there and here is a horn-rim egghead with four suitcases wants to go to Cal Tech in Pasadena.

"So we start. He asks how things are around here and I tell him it couldn't be better. I reverse everything about L.A., see? He talks smog, I talk clear blue skies. He talks crowded freeways, I talk speed. It gets to be a game. He's watchin' the meter and he asks how's tips. Well, I tell him tips is *fantastic.* Last guy gimme over ten bucks, I tell him, because I didn't think he'd believe it was thirteen-fourteen. Well, he don't want to be a piker, and when we get to Cal Tech he shells out the fare, which is plenty, and then adds three silver dollars. He's been to Las Vegas. How's that for wonderful? Next I go to the Green Hotel, four cabs in line, but right away a convention comes out, and I get a happy drunk wants to go to the Coliseum. He's happy-plastered, see, and loaded with dough. I give him the business, and by now I'm singin' like a canary on a sunny morning and—oh, well, that's the way it's been. Couldn't be better, except for Sarah."

"Didn't you tell her about this?"

"Doc, how can I? I come in whistlin' and she says: 'Look out, kids, he's drunk.' And I'm sober as a owl. It makes me sore. Then I shell out some dough on the table for her to buy herself a British raincoat she's always wanted and she says I been shootin' craps again. Doc, my blood boils, see? I can look on the bright side away from Sarah, but at home, *bro-ther!* It's like one fella I had, astronomer, went all the way up Mt. Wilson—man, what a pretty ride—smells good, too—sage—well, he had trouble with *his* wife, see? He said it was a 'failure of communercation.' How's that for sayin' it eleganto, doc? That's what I got with Sarah—no communercation. By now I froze up, and *she* froze up! I go outa the house mornin's tap-dancin' and singin', to get into the mood, y'know, and she thinks I got plastered durin' breakfast, she can't see how, but I musta! That's her attitude—one hunnerd per cent negative. I want you to call her up, doc. Tell her it wasn't no crap game. Tell her it's just this old Jewish philosophy, up to date."

"When did you last take Sarah out to dinner, Julius?"

"*Out* to dinner? You mean—*out,* like Chinese food?"

"Take her alone, without the kids? I recommend it. And when the candles are lit and you've ordered her favorite dinner, tell her all about this—tell her the truth."

"She ain't speakin' to me."

"Now you're being negative."

"Well, I'm speakin'. But she ain't."

"I never knew a woman who didn't like to go out to dinner. No dishes, no planning."

"I dunno, doc. I tried explainin' this affirmative stuff to my best buddy at the garage, and he thinks I'm nuts."

"Sarah will listen. You've already let your example show what's happened. She must secretly be puzzled. Do you know the story of Aladdin's lamp?"

He'd never heard it. So I told him, and gave him the metaphysical interpretation. He didn't quite get it.

"Now, don't tell anybody but Sarah. You reversed your thinking outside. It will work at home, too, Julius. It works everywhere."

"Does, huh?" he said thoughtfully. "You mean—polite, the whole bit, hold out her chair and all?" Suddenly he beamed at me. "Okay, I'm gonna try it t'night."

Mrs. Julius Podholz was in the line at the Wiltern when I stood out front shaking hands after the service on Sunday. Her accent matched Julius', cadence for cadence. She was a perky little woman in a new topcoat which she planned to shorten later; she'd only bought it yesterday.

"It's reversible," she explained, and smiled nervously. "Like Julius Podholz."

We stepped aside after the crowd had thinned. She was excited.

"Doctor," she said, as if it were too good to be true, "it's like I had two husbands, see? With the best one on the inside, yeah? Now it's Julius Podholz turned inside out like before we was married. It's a miracle. He takes me to Chan T'su's Cafe, and at first he sounds a little crazy, about Aladdin's lamp, and a Law we didn't know about, and how being polite is part of love, and brings good reactions. Pretty soon I gotta *believe* him. He's kinda shinin'. He says it's even worked at *home,* because look at us talkin'. He wants I should read up on philosophy and tell him more about it. Julius ain't what you'd call a fast reader."

We made an office appointment. I warned her that the rest of the way might not be as easy. It is a curious fact, which each discovers in his own fashion, that the evidentials, the coincidences, the answers to prayer, come tumbling over one another in the beginnning and then, once you're thoroughly convinced, suddenly there's work to do—and dry periods, too, until, sometimes, like the monk with the aching knees, the most devout find themselves saying: "I believe, help thou my unbelief."

"That's okay with me," Mrs. Podholz said. "We never had it easy. It used to be I could just bust down and cry, Julius changed so since we got married. But now I found out he's reversible I got hope, doctor. We got a fine family, y'know, four sweet kids. Julius loves 'em—and now he's gonna let it show."

Sitting on the stool in Ernest's kitchen Sunday after church, I told him the story while he cut thick slices of hickory-smoked ham and supervised the baking of the beans which Lena had prepared the night before. He wore an apron made of hopsacking which Hazel had bought in Mexico. It had a high front bib and was too big for him but he was sentimental about it and wouldn't have it shortened.

"Mrs. Podholz arrived a little late for the service," I said, concluding the anecdote. "We had standing room only. She stood at the back of the theater all during church."

It was a chance to resume the debate. He ignored it. I went on:

"Lately, when I think about all the thousands of people

who would help us build an edifice, I feel as if one word would move a mountain."

He eyed me gravely.

"No faith?"

"Faith, yes. It hasn't yet produced a shovel, but it will. That is, with your help. You can say the Word." I pressed on, "How many did *you* turn away today?"

"Didn't ask."

"At the Wiltern we had eighty or so who didn't care to stand. That's fewer than usual. Perhaps people are getting discouraged after being turned away so often."

He opened the oven, tested a spoonful of beans, approved and closed the oven door again. Then he surprised me.

"This morning a woman asked me if I'd ever chauffeured for children," he said. "I was obliged to admit I hadn't. She told me chauffeuring was now a big part of many a woman's life. She asked if I believed in Sunday school, and I said most certainly, our sort. I said it's a blessing for youngsters to be brought up in faith, not fear. Then she asked me why I made it so difficult for all the people with children when they'd be willing to help us build a place of our own."

I held my breath. He didn't look at me.

"How much would it cost to buy the property next door?" he asked.

"A hundred and sixty thousand." I could tell him to the penny.

"Suppose I'd shuffled off and you had a four- or five-hundred-thousand-dollar mortgage—you'd discharge the obligation?"

"You know I would."

"That first night in San Francisco the sky was an inverted bowl with stars shining through." He faced me now. "There's no reason the edifice couldn't remind us of Emerson's 'heaven and earth for its beams and rafters.' I'd like to see a building that didn't look like a church—round—no beginning, no end, like the Allness of God. We'll enter across grass and through a garden. Over the sanctuary let's have a blue ceiling to represent the sky with stars shining—"

I embraced him.

"Yes, Bill, yes." He used his handkerchief mightily. "Hazel loved good music. She was an artist in her own right, you know." He was seeing it now: "There must be a magnificent organ—"

"The Hazel Holmes Memorial Organ!"

I waited through a long pause.

"If they would," he said at last, tucking the handkerchief back in his hip pocket, "we'd be proud." Then he leveled a finger: "My original dream must be built, too, and on the same theme: a teaching and publishing center, a world headquarters—" He described a harmonious group of modern buildings—"That's right, the sanctuary first—the healing consciousness—" planning always excited him; but now suddenly he broke off. "When it's finished, whether I'm around or not, you'll keep the ritual simple and beautiful—at the absolute minimum—won't you, Bill?"

9

That Last Cigarette—and Easy Does It!

A half million, eight hundred and forty-seven cigarettes after my first furtive Omar at age fourteen I decided to use a little will power and quit smoking.

Will power isn't the way to do it.

All was anguish.

Seven days later a nervous committee from my own household, including a starchy toddler, waited upon me with three packs of cork-tips. They begged me to start again. My next-door neighbor, a doctor, was fascinated by the withdrawal symptoms and said I couldn't have suffered more if I'd been smoking hashish.

I was hooked.

I'd worked my way up to sixty stubbed out cigarettes a day by this time—smoked before breakfast, all day long at the typewriter, woke up to smoke in the night and—always —lit up before answering the phone. The very height of discipline.

The first person singular, as you have guessed, has now been adopted by Dr. Hornaday's co-author, one-time newspaperman, one-time atheist, later agnostic, never a man of the cloth. It is necessary, briefly, to assume this responsibility because I wish to trace, step by step, a metaphysical *healing* which is something entirely different than stopping smoking or quitting cigarettes. It was so remarkable in its total effect, and so painless when finally accomplished, that a properly written account of the experience may be useful to some other compulsive who wishes he could quit but has learned that will power isn't the answer. Any normal man or woman has enough *will power* to quit. There's nothing to that. You quit and suffer. You nobly put away the favorite lighter, toss a half pack into the fireplace, and devote twenty-four hours a day to wondering whether it's worthwhile to go on living; this continues for a couple of weeks and then the pain ceases and, finally, you gradually return to balance and begin to get a little work done. But you've only *quit*. You're always in danger. A couple of puffs after a drink or after dinner or, particularly, after breakfast, and you're gone again.

A *healing* is different.

It is habit surgery.

There are reflexes and fetishes which have to be done away with after forty years or so of thoroughly enjoying cigarettes. Well, no—in my case about thirty-seven years. During the last period I tried, off and on, to lay off because my throat was raw most of the time, and my cough alarmed some people, including two live-and-let-live characters with whom I made a trip down the Inland Waterway on a motor cruiser called the *Karoo*.

All this was part of it: my lighter boasted a club crest,

and I loved it and kept it in a certain pocket. Like Queeg's steel balls in the *Caine Mutiny,* the smoothness of the metal was a comfort under my thumb in times of crisis. And never in all the years at the typewriter had I inserted a sheet of paper into the machine without the reassuring spiral of smoke rising from an ashtray nearby. Or *two* reassuring spirals when the flow was on.

All this had to be done away with—all the reflexes, all the fetishes.

And it was.

And I couldn't tell you when it happened.

Now, I am the only one who can know for sure what a miracle this was. You'll believe me, I hope, because I wouldn't take your time or mine in a book such as this to fabricate the story. In the eight years I was trying to cut down, I'd read of metaphysical healings, but the words didn't convey much meaning. Nobody had ever traced through the steps in print, so far as I knew, and the words were flat on the page. Since then I've talked to several men and women who have had similar experiences; the beginning and the end are the same but the personal adventures which led to *belief* are, of course, greatly varied.

It begins, as Ernest Holmes would say, *within.*

It begins with a *belief* that a healing is possible.

And how anyone else will arrive at this is an exceedingly personal matter. Perhaps it will start with a series of Capital C Coincidences preceded by reading in the metaphysical field. It will call for the use of techniques which are simpler than you expect them to be and which will not run counter to your religion, I was going to say "if you have one," but you will have one before you're through, or you won't be healed. And *religion* is the word; not theology.

If you enjoy smoking as my wife Ruthie does, and it doesn't hurt you—and it doesn't hurt Ruthie—you may skip this chapter. But if you're among the new millions who secretly or openly wish they could get it over with in a reasonably painless fashion, you're invited to attend.

We'll go step by step, following a series of small miracles along the way. Because in the process of gathering the *belief* necessary to the healing we saw boulders moved in what was—unless we are all out of our minds—a metaphysical demonstration; we, ourselves, bought a house that wasn't for sale with money from a house that couldn't be sold; and I learned to use the subjective mind in a direct and definite way. And it was faith in *this* technique—and the larger faith implied—which made the surgery possible.

Now, then, the beginning: one summer day on Orcas Island I stopped my car for a closer inspection of a roadside weed called Queen Anne's lace. Here was architectural structure so delicately balanced, so superbly wrought, that each supporting stem carried the artist's signature: *God*. An accident in nature? Nonsense. Accidents are not graceful; accidents do not produce beauty and an environment for beauty; accidents do not create intelligent design. That pause at the roadside led gradually to all sorts of wonders hitherto taken for granted, and to a sense of central relationship—all were one. The problem of good and evil would have to be explained in another dimension, if such existed; too many choices were possible in a world of too many mysteries, and it was time to choose: an Ultimate Intelligence had produced beauty and the miracle of consciousness to appreciate the beauty, and what was this but Love and Law?

That was step one.

We had been reading in metaphysics; some writers were tortuously obscure, producing upside-down sentences with terrible labor, and some were permanently over our heads but one man in his serene conviction of a universe o Ultimate Good dared to be clear the first time he tried. Dr. Holmes spoke right out.

Along in here somewhere our youngest, in pinafore, white gloves, and with prayer book, came steaming out of Sunday school, on hell and damnation Sunday, never to go back.

"Daddy, I don't *believe* it!" Ciji said. "I'm never, *never* going there again."

She'd been around a very short time in her bobby sox and starchy dresses, but she looked mature that morning.

"What happened, Ceeg?"

"Sandra has polio. She's three years old. Do you think Sandra sinned—and God gave her polio?"

"I most certainly do not."

"The teacher said that's what happened—Sandra was being punished for sins. And I don't think there's any hell, either. I'm going to find a more cheerful Sunday school."

And there it was. Joy, our elder daughter, had already explored the countryside and settled on a more cheerful Sunday school. A beloved church, which had sustained the family for generations, was lost in the Middle Ages and these youngsters instinctively rejected the blighting effect of an outworn theology.

A little child shall lead them into metaphysics.

And that was step two.

That the subjective mind may be consciously directed and definitely used was proved to me at a time when, professionally, such demands were made on my powers of invention—the writing of eighteen half-hour radio shows in eighteen days, for instance—that I had to have help from *somewhere.*

That some work could be done while asleep I had learned years before when writing a show of my own, but that definite techniques might be employed was news to me. In the early days of radio I had written for several years *The College Inn Comedy* six times each week, and later *The Bartons* five times each week, and I had a lot of characters padding around inside my skull. When waking in the middle of the night—3 A.M. usually—to sit at the window and smoke the cigarette which would get me through until morning, I'd often find that my subconscious mind had been putting together tomorrow's script. It was always a pleasant surprise. But that there was a way politely to *order* myself to do this I didn't so much as suspect.

Nearly everyone has had the experience of awakening moments before the alarm clock rings. With practice almost anybody can "set his mind" to rouse at a certain hour and, if confident, then can spend the night in deep repose and awaken exactly on time. Isn't this, in itself, a wonder? The phrase "Let me sleep on it" is as old as man. (We, the authors of this book, personally know a woman who dreamt that she was looking at an X ray of the bones in her own neck, and later her description of the dream led her doctors to the discovery—after years of failure—of the cause of her persistent pain.)

Techniques for using the subjective mind are now practiced professionally by many people. The gifted Mary Austin, novelist, essayist and folklorist, made a study of the creative impulse and in 1928 published her findings in the book *Everyman's Genius* which, unhappily, has long been out of print. She used the phrase "we can know what we do not know," and for me it was a long step toward *belief* when I found this to be literally true.

The experience which stands out most vividly in my memory I'll call step three:

Midway through the writing of a novel, my personal auditor—a lady who handles her own dripping oar in this unsteady skiff—suggested putting the book aside to write eight short stories. She had peered into the future—upcoming college tuition, insurance, taxes, *you* know—and she allowed as how eight short stories, if they all sold instantly to the *Post,* might possibly rescue us. The *Post* of that period was a great boon to writers; the editors scheduled four short stories each week, were always on the lookout for serials, made up their minds in three days and mailed the check at once.

So! With a backlog of material recently gathered while lecturing on the chicken patty circuit I began to write a little number called "Orchids at Noon," in which I planned to use a line recently tossed off by my painter friend John Hilton, about a lady, size 48: "She stood closer to me than I did to her."

"Orchids at Noon" became unmanageable early in the effort, so one morning I went for a stiff hike on my favorite Mt. Wilson trail above Sierra Madre—we were living in nearby Arcadia at the time. The fire laws were strict and I couldn't smoke up there and that was good for me.

I was climbing a firebreak in a state of mind as close to unthinking as I've ever been, when suddenly a story about modern China, and a young man on a sampan, dropped into my head. It was amazing. In my mind's eye I saw a stout American businessman toss a silver dollar, and the boy dove into the water for it. "There but for the grace of God go I—" the American thought, and wished that he might guide the boy in a wise use of the dollar in those days of inflation.

I started back down the mountain with the rest of the story tumbling into my mind.

Nobody knows less about China than I do. I'd recently read in the press that blood was flowing, "agrarian reformers" had taken over, and that the inflation was out of hand. I'd never been in the Orient or near it. But when the writing began, the narrative fell into cadence as if being translated from the Chinese, and when the story appeared, my mail was unusual and from Far East places. A China hand, en route to safety, came upon that week's issue of the Post and was moved to write at length. One man who had escaped to New York thought he remembered me from the good old days in Shanghai; a Chinese teen-ager wrote from Australia assuring me that his parents had indeed clung to the old ways too long; an expert complained that the name "Hoy Toy" probably would not be found among people on sampans—only then did I realize that approving letters were coming from people who knew more about my subject than I did! Scholarship would blow my cursory research out of the water, I have no doubt; but the tale must have been true in essence for its day. I do know that a curious atmosphere existed in my study during the work and some of the narrative surprised me.

Now, then. There is nothing mysterious about this—beyond the fact that consciousness itself is a mystery; when we get ourselves out of the way and allow the deep self to function, *we can know what we do not know.*

Ernest Holmes put it very clearly. And since his exposition was part of the healing process let me quote from *Science of Mind:*

> Since the individual subjective mind is the storehouse of memory, it retains all that the eye has seen, the ear heard, or the mentality conceived. Since it contains much that the outer man never consciously knew, and is the receptacle of much of the race knowledge through unconscious communication, it must (and does) have a knowledge that far surpasses the objective faculties.
>
> Realizing that the subjective draws to itself everything that it is in sympathy with, we see that anyone who is sympathetically inclined toward the race, or vibrates to the race-thought, might pick up the entire race-emotion and experience and—if he were able to bring it to the surface—could consciously depict it. Many of the world's orators, actors and writers have been able to do this, which explains why some of them have been so erratic, for they have been more or less controlled by the emotions which they have contacted.
>
> Anyone contacting the subjective side of the race-mentality, with the ability to bring it to the surface, will have at his disposal an emotional knowledge that many lifetimes of hard study could not accumulate. But IF ONE HAD TO SURRENDER HIS INDIVIDUALITY IN THE PROCESS, HE WOULD BETTER REMAIN IGNORANT.
>
> There is, of course, a much deeper seat of knowledge than the subjective mind, which is the Spirit; direct contact with the Spirit is Illumination.

There is a law in operation here because everyone's experience is essentially the same. Last summer in a hillside studio near his hidden-away house in a Beverly Hills canyon, I saw James Cagney's unforgettable painting of a boxer. It is executed in varying shades of red, a brutal face with a mass of old scar tissue and new wounds—and, in contrast, a pale, slim white hand, with starched cuffs and golden cuff links, lifting the gloved fist of The Winnah. The comment is complete.

Cagney has retired from the screen and now exercises his other talents, writes sparkling verse, shown only to his friends, and paints with grace and skill, approaching each subject with the same acute observation and wry humor which characterized his acting. Because *The Winnah* struck me as one of those special performances never to be repeated, and because Cagney will figure in another aspect of this chapter, I asked if he could remember what went on in his mind while the picture was being painted. He writes:

"My reaction is this: if you can describe what happens that ain't it. The compulsion to put down something beyond the usual, beyond what we already know, triggers a flow which was not in one's ken a moment before. Where it comes from, who knows? *The Winnah* painted itself. I don't remember thinking too much where I was going next; only when something didn't look right did I awaken briefly to a technical problem, and it was solved impatiently in order to get the job done while the heat was on."

Many another painter would give similar testimony but Mr. Cagney has a double claim on this chapter because he is crowded to the ears with medical lore—he has two brothers who are doctors—and once vividly described for me the inside of a smoker's lungs in contrast to the sunrise beauty of normal lung tissue. We were in the Dismal Swamp Canal at the time, sitting at the stern of a sturdy motor cruiser, the *Karoo,* in the soft autumn sunshine. I'd had a bit of a coughing spell.

"How many cigarettes d'you suppose you've smoked up

to now, H?" he asked mildly. He does his bends, doesn't smoke and is a disciplined, gifted, public-spirited, admirable fella. "Must be in the millions!"

Forty years, an average of at least forty a day—what a cloud! Even our fellow traveler on that Waterway jaunt, the seagoing Jim McDaniel, who crumpled an empty pack every evening, had glumly decided that my performance was excessive and dangerous. These two had no interest in metaphysics; their suggestion was to "kick it out."

However, the statistics stayed with me and must go down as step four.

It seems, looking back, that it's necessary to erase the anthropomorphic concepts and approach with an open mind the metaphysical point of view. These words from *Science of Mind* present one aspect clearly.

> Experience has taught us that the subjective tendency of this intelligent Law of creative force may consciously be directed and definitely used. This is the greatest discovery of all time.

This is true, and it is most effective when accompanied by belief.

But how does one acquire belief?

In my experience it comes to some of us a glimmer at a time.

Ernest Holmes used to tell the story of an unfortunate sailor who was washed overboard from a freighter in the turbulent tides beyond the Golden Gate one stormy winter night. The seaman found himself utterly alone, dog-paddling against a backwash which was swiftly carrying him seaward. The situation was desperate. He yelled skyward:

"God, look. Get me out of this and I'll quit smoking."

It was a tawdry offer—he'd planned to quit smoking, anyway. Sensing this, he shouted:

"And *drinking,* God. I'll give up all booze, including beer."

A wave washed into his open mouth.

Then the tide tumbled him heels over head, and when he again beheld the night sky, he bellowed:

"I'll get me a *wife.* I'll raise a Christian family. I'll send 'em all to church!" And then he screamed, going whole hog: "I'll go myself. *God, save me and all the rest of my life I'll live like a saint!"*

A giant redwood log appeared on the crest of a wave and coasted down toward him.

"Never mind, God," he yelled, as he hurled a leg over it, and found himself riding on the inshore tide toward the warm lights of shore. *"The deal's off. I found myself a log!"*

It was a tale out of the old church, of course, but Ernest made it a parable for the new. He illustrated his point with a quote from Emerson: "Prayer is the soliloquy of a jubilant and beholding soul." In other words, the sailor, receptive, in a state of need, *beheld* the log. Jesus repeatedly told his followers that the Kingdom of Heaven is here *now.* Few understood him then or later. In our self-created desperation many of us—Ernest would say—are too terrified and self-absorbed to behold an ever-available avenue of escape!

Unless my eyes deceive me, church attendance is made up predominantly of those who have been softened up by experience. In churches of various denominations all across the country we have seen a disproportion of mature people. Once upon a time in sophomoric scorn of my elders I proclaimed that it was fear of the tomb which sent these ancients churchward of a Sunday morning. The years led me to amend the attitude and to apologize. With my own growing list of evidentials it's now clear that many other seekers have experienced wonders in an ever-expanding understanding of the spiritual universe.

And here then is step five—my own particular evidentials which led to *belief*. Every student you encounter will have his own; these are true incidents in my own search and are presented here in order to dramatize what to Bernard Opley was merely mishmash:

An astonishing incident led me wholly to accept a remark of Ernest's in *Science of Mind:*

> The simplest way to state the proposition is to say that we have a conscious mind that operates within a subjective field, which is creative. The conscious mind is Spirit, the subjective mind is Law.

An example, a true account:

A mile or so north of La Jolla, California, there's a hidden, one-lane gravel road which follows a natural course through a cypress grove to a cottage on a cliff. Even with explicit directions the road is difficult to find.

The cottage once had been the home of a collector of Indian artifacts, a folklorist, but now it was the property of Frank and Helen Meredith. Frank had been an oil company executive and was now retired; Helen was a professional practitioner of spiritual healing. They became intimate friends of ours.

You'll recall, I hope, Bernard Opley's observation that an interest in metaphysics mysteriously brings metaphysicians into one's life. We first encountered Frank and

Helen Meredith in a church; when they bought and rebuilt the cottage near La Jolla, we were invited to visit them during our summer holiday.

One lovely July morning we drove south along the coast from Arcadia and, with map in hand, managed to miss the Merediths' road. A postman set us right. A rough double lane wound through rocks and shrubbery to an attractive newly painted white cottage on the cliff overlooking the sea. We found Frank and two husky Mexican gardeners stripped to the waist engaged in a formidable project. Several boulders which once had complimented the folklorist's modest house were now, obviously, misfits on the landscape. Helen had voted for a flower garden and white picket fence. The gardeners were optimists. They had discovered a watercourse which ran into a gully and so into the sea; it should have been a simple matter to roll the boulders down to the surf. The rocks wouldn't budge, though. One of them was shoulder-high. A shovel handle snapped like a gunshot as we drove up.

Later, when we had unpacked, we inspected the pitful scratchings around the boulders. Helen quoted:

". . . Verily, I say unto you, if ye have faith as a grain of mustard seed, ye shall say unto this mountain, Remove hence to yonder place; and it shall remove; and nothing shall be impossible unto you."

"Matthew 17:20." Frank grinned. "Why didn't we think of this before?"

"I'll get busy," Helen said.

Ruth and I exchanged glances. They couldn't be serious! Helen would have said our memory was short. She had once "spoken the Word" for Ruth during a murderous assault by a bad anchovy which turned up in a four-dollar

Caesar salad. The healing had been an astonishing, *instant,* capital C Coincidence which flabbergasted me. I had been a much-worried eyewitness—"Why—why—why! I'm all right now!" Ruthie had said. But this! Surely they were going pretty far. Helen, a beautiful and otherwise rational woman, went cheerfully off to her study to go to work. We sat on the front steps talking politics with Frank; away from religious subjects he was a hardheaded and sensible man.

In a few hours we had forgotten the conversation, and a couple of mornings later a load of topsoil was brought in and unloaded. Frank decided to make a garden around the boulders. Imaginative planting with vines and dwarf cypress would take away the raw look, and it mightn't be necessary to remove the boulders, after all. They'd gradually diminish under greenery. And how was that for metaphysics?

In the midafternoon, sailboats from San Diego harbor were rounding a marker a mile or so beyond our shores and I borrowed binoculars and went up to the old redwood arbor near the cliff's edge for a better view.

A few minutes later a car drove in and stopped in the turnaround just below me. A well-dressed elderly man, with glasses of his own, apologized for intruding—his youngest daughter and his son-in-law were in the race, he said, and he hadn't been able to see the north marker from the highway.

The Merediths and Ruthie joined us—there were no introductions—and we watched until the sails were skimming south again. The gentleman thanked us for allowing the intrusion and went down toward his car.

Then he went beyond it and walked all the way around the largest boulder.

"I was just wondering," he said, retracing his steps, "if you people have any special fondness for those rocks?"

"None," said Helen promptly.

"In fact, we're planning to get rid of them," Frank said, startled. "Why?"

"I could certainly use the larger ones. I'm building a very unusual house across the cove."

Ruth and I found ourselves staring at each other.

"You'd use them for *fill?*" asked Frank.

"Oh, no. It's a house with lots of glass, you see—very modern. My architect asked me to keep my eyes open for some big rocks. They plan to use white pebbles, a couple of dwarf evergreens and tall, stark rocks in the front yard."

By now we all avoided looking at one another.

"You're welcome to all of these," Helen said unsteadily.

"I wouldn't need them *all*—" He hesitated, then added generously, "but I'll haul 'em away for you if you like as long as we'll have the men and machinery here. . . ."

I began to ask reporter's questions. When had the architect spoken to him about this? *This morning!* How had he discovered the gravel road? *He had parked not too far away to watch the race—the road was right there.* He was puzzled. Why all the excitement?

"Mrs. Meredith will tell you," I said.

"After he's hauled the rocks away," Helen laughed.

And Ruth said, "Pinch me."

When the gentleman had gone, promising to return tomorrow with trucks and workmen, we probed for Helen's technique. What sort of "work" had she done? She thought back. She had centered her thinking on a phrase: "Faith is the substance of things hoped for, the evidence of things not seen." Then she had explored further: "Faith should enlarge its borders. This is no longer the place for the boulders; if there's a more suitable place, it shall be revealed to us." That evening she found Frank studying the want ads. Sometimes builders announced a need for "fill." That seemed logical enough. They then decided to watch for such ads. But nothing helpful turned up in the paper and then, busy with other things, they forgot to look again.

When he heard the story, the gentleman from across the cove thought it was an interesting coincidence. He wasn't too impressed. But *I* was impressed. Lighting one cigarette on another, I was now also hooked on metaphysics.

A few days later we packed for home. By now we carried a traveler's bookcase crowded with such offbeat reading as Plotinus, Pico della Mirandola—the fifteenth-century prodigy whose open-minded search for God reminded me of the young Ernest Holmes—Ouspensky, Troward, Mrs. Eddy, *The Letters of the Scattered Brotherhood* and, always, *Science of Mind.* On Pages 87 and 88 of the latter I found a paragraph which might explain what happened in the case of the boulders; at any rate, Ernest's words held special luminosity for me on that particular day:

> There is no such thing as your mind, my mind and God's Mind. There is only Mind, in which we all "live and move and have our being."
>
> Things are ideas in form. What else could they be? There is nothing from which to make things except ideas. In the beginning, we behold nothing visible; there is only an Infinite Possibility, a Limitless Imagination, a Consciousness—the only action of this Consciousness being Idea.
>
> That which we call *our* subjective mind is, in reality, our

identity in Infinite Mind. It is the result of our mental attitudes. It is our mental atmosphere, or center, in Universal Subjective Mind, in which are retained all of the images, impressions, inherited tendencies and race suggestions. We see then that our subjective mind is the *medium* through which experiences come to us.

We were not the same two people who had driven to La Jolla a few days before. Step number five had been a long one—more than a coincidence, surely; how much evidence would we need before we began with confidence to work out problems in this astonishing fashion?

"We could start now," Ruthie said.

As we approached the city, we began our shallow breathing and I asked:

"How do you 'treat' for smog?"

That was the summer a freak pressure pushed clouds of smog into San Gabriel Valley and held it there; a slow stirring of hot currents sent it up against Mt. Wilson but then lacked force to push it up and over. It blanketed the countryside for days, and the foothill towns gasped beneath it. One blistering morning, with too much carbon monoxide in the tobacco smoke, I phoned my neighbor who was chairman of the Bring Industry to California Committee and, in some memorable phrases, bade him good-by forever. Then we closed our once-beloved house and headed four hundred miles north.

Carmel, on the Monterey Peninsula, is a unique, embattled haven, remnant of a gentler century. There are no neon signs. It has a mile-long sandy beach without lifeguard, Ferris wheel or hot dog stand. The tumultuous icy tides would rip off a bikini, and summers are often cold and foggy. Away from Ocean Avenue the streets are pitch-black at night and a true Carmelite quickly becomes an uncomplaining member of the "flashlight set." The village originally was settled by artists and writers and so has no house numbers; a man with an unlisted phone and a locked gate can get a lot of work done. Citizens must talk it over with the city council before they cut down a parkway tree. But best of all is the air.

The air is so pure that it gives cigarettes the cool, sweet taste you hear about in the TV ads.

We rented a typical Carmel house—redwood, board-and-batten—and settled into the chores.

Carlton E. Morse's radio show, *One Man's Family,* for which I was writing, had now passed its twentieth year on the air and would go for seven more. We were sometimes condescended to as a "soap opera," which we were not; the shows were written, acted and produced to the best of our several abilities, and with respect for an audience which looked upon the family as actually existing; we couldn't afford mistakes in attitude or relationships.

The village turned out to be the perfect place to work. And play. After our daughters joined us, at the end of summer school and camp, we decided to sell the house in the smog and buy one in Carmel.

"The house we really want isn't for sale," Ruthie told the girls, "but we're trying to figure out how you would solve the problem metaphysically."

"Does the owner like his house?"

"It's Mrs. Gridley. She loves it."

"It wouldn't be right to move her out, would it?"

"Probably not."

"And who would want ours in the smog?"

"That's what we wonder."

We had fallen in love with a rambling redwood cottage on a rise overlooking the river, bay and Point Lobos; the living room had a spectacular view, and the study had none, which was perfect. There were four bedrooms, a patio with a flagstone wall, a gate with a lock. Mrs. Gertrude Gridley, who had followed the Barbours on the air for twenty years and was bothered by suspense factors we'd forgotten about, had invited us for tea.

"Oh, dear, no!" she said when we asked if her house was ever for rent. "I wouldn't think of renting it, or selling it, either. It was rebuilt last year, you know—it's the house I need for my antiques."

Thomas Jefferson had slept in one of the beds and John Hancock in another. Napoleon had kept his shirts in the highboy. Mrs. Gridley and a yellow cat were guarding the heirlooms until the time came to pass them along to nieces and nephews.

We looked at other houses, but without much enthusiasm, and decided at the end of August to go home, sell our house, and come back, be sensible, and find something we could afford to buy.

Now there's this about metaphysicians: they'll pass you along from one to another like a torch. Helen Meredith put us in touch with Mrs. Daisy Haven, a Carmel realtor—if "realtor" is the right gender—and she delighted in the challenge. What a problem! What a *delicious* problem.

"Now let's be affirmative!" cried Mrs. Haven, a lean, wondrously healthy Carmelite who walked the beach before breakfast every morning. "First things first, my dears. Go sell *your* house and come back. I know Gert Gridley's place; I sold it to her. We may find something you like even better."

In Pasadena, she said, there was a young metaphysician named Larry Simmons, a real estate expert.

"He operates on a very high principle," announced Mrs. Haven. "He's just the man for you. I'll write him tonight."

"How does a man of high principle sell houses in the smog?" we wondered.

This stopped her briefly.

"Well, there *has* to be a way," she decided brightly. "There's an answer to everything. Now, we can't afford to think in negative terms, can we? The answer is always here, you know, in time; when we treat properly, our understanding unfolds and we behold the solution."

It got a little heavy for me—I'm allergic to the fixed smile of some metaphysicians—but she was a charmer and she left us with hope.

"Now, never force a demonstration," she said gaily, as we prepared to drive away. "Let it all unfold. You'll be in good hands when you get home."

We needed any help we could get. Not only were the FOR SALE signs bristling in the midday gloom, but a number of neighbors had locked up their houses and fled to the beach. Even atheists were praying for a wind. Disturbing headlines announced a smog-alert, and one radio announcer told all prospective buyers and the world at large: "The pressure area continues to press down on the foothill communities, and certain sections are experiencing something like a London fog."

Out of the London fog came Mr. Larry Simmons. He turned up the second morning wearing a tailor-made seersucker and driving a British sports car. An eastern school plus two years of Harvard Business had made him easy in his shoes. He'd been a student of metaphysics all his life, he said, and how was Daisy? He was affirmative, lacked the fixed smile and we liked him.

"There's one reason the houses around here aren't selling," he told us flatly. "They're overpriced. If you expect four times what you have invested, it'll take a while. Three times, considering the inflation, would seem fair. Any objection to setting an honest price?"

"That sounds breathtakingly novel," we agreed.

He grinned. "My grandfather has a saying about the stock market—bears make money, bulls make money, but pigs always lose. It's true in real estate, too. Over the years we've found it wise to accept the first reasonable offer. Oh, we'll set a trading cushion; it's expected, it's part of the waltz, but if we get a fair offer, we should take it."

"While we're being so honest," I said, "what do you tell 'em about the smog?"

"I'm sure you wouldn't sell the place to some poor unsuspecting ex-GI from Iowa on a clear day—not without a warning. But I don't worry about that. There are plenty of people who actually like smog."

"Quit kidding."

"No, no, you find them everywhere. Pay attention at a cocktail party. One man will say, 'Oh, the smog isn't bad where I live.' And another one will tell you: 'Why, we hardly notice it.' You listen—you'll hear it."

"Why, I have heard it!" Ruthie exclaimed. "But I thought they had leather lungs or were out of their minds."

"It actually doesn't bother some people when business is good," he told us. "Ask 'em what line they're in—and usually they have a vested interest in the smog. Maybe they crack gasoline. Or build backyard incinerators. Or sell cars."

"In other words," Ruth mused, "if they know about it, and defend it, we are free of moral obligation?"

"Why not? The other man's motives are no concern of ours as long as we're honest with him. Now, then. You don't have a swimming pool. We'll consider that an asset."

"Everybody told us it was a liability," I said.

"People with small children will prefer the badminton court." Mr. Simmons made a note. "We'll advertise—affirming it—badminton court, no swimming pool. Now, then, can we agree on a price?"

We knew what the house had cost, he figured the inflation and added a thousand dollars for a trading cushion.

"A good businessman's first offer will be fifteen hundred less than the asking price," he said. "You can then haggle over five hundred if you care to. But I wouldn't, neither would my Dad, neither would Gramps."

"Are they metaphysicians, too?" Ruth wondered.

"Gramps is," he said. "We used to go clear over to the Wiltern theater every Sunday to hear Dr. Holmes lecture. Gramps says it's the most sensible way to approach problems. It's made a big difference to us."

"I can see where it might."

He had brought along a FOR SALE sign in his MG, and he posted it in the ivy on the parkway.

When I woke up at three o'clock that morning to blow smoke out the window into the smog, I was actually feeling hopeful.

The next day a young matron wandered in about lunchtime. She seemed strangely excited after she had looked around and went away to get her husband. Her name was Betty Ambercrombie. She had four children under eight. "Roger will be delighted to know you don't have a swimming pool," she beamed.

At one o'clock she phoned us from her husband's desk to say they'd come by at five-thirty.

She confessed that my office, a separate building with bedroom, bath and fireplace, would be perfect for her mother-in-law, who lived with them.

"Has anybody else been looking at it?" she inquired anxiously.

"Only one other woman."

"Oh, *dear.* Don't do anything until my husband sees it."

Mr. Roger Ambercrombie obviously was a young man going somewhere. When he arrived in his bow tie and three-piece Dacron, the place had never looked better. A four o'clock breeze had cleared away a patch of smog, and for the first time in days we could see a firebreak on Mt. Wilson. Our front sprinklers had been turned off when they arrived and the lawn, trees and shrubbery wore that sparkling, washed-down professional-gardener look. I found myself a little choked up; almost hated to sell it.

Mr. Ambercrombie took a brisk, sharp-eyed turn around the place. While his wife talked to Ruthie, who impulsively threw in the freezer, the dining room table, eight chairs and the drapes, Mr. Ambercrombie came crisply to a decision.

"Well, I like it," he said. "I could put a narrow asphalt walk around the orchard for the tricycles." He offered me fifteen hundred dollars less than the asking price.

"Now hold on," I said nobly. "This I must tell you. The

smog has been horrible lately. It backs up against the mountain, can't get over and—"

"Smog?" snapped the young businessman impatiently. "People have a fixation about smog. This country is *growing,* man. We're a big industrial complex. Fortunes are being made. Smog doesn't bother *me.* And Betty and the kids don't mind it, either. Smog is more or less a state of mind. Besides, it's all over the world. Been in Tokyo lately?"

I was fascinated.

"What business are you in, Mr. Ambercrombie?"

"Car wash business," he told me briskly. "I've patented the machinery—have nine places now and expect to build twenty more in California alone. Well, have we got a deal?"

For appearances' sake I went into the waltz. I countered. He countered. I said: Sold!

Mr. Simmons wasn't surprised. He said he'd drive out and take the FOR SALE sign down in the morning.

The neighbors were stunned.

"How in the world did you sell it so *quickly?*" someone asked.

"Oh," said Ruthie vaguely, "it was all kind of a coincidence, I guess."

We all wept when we drove away. A gentle all-night rain had cleared the skies. Sunlight gleamed on the Mt. Wilson Observatory, and every breath of the cool air was a delight. We dared not glance back as we rolled out of the driveway. We were homeless.

But that had been step number six.

"Let's try to understand the technique," Ruthie said.

"Each problem is different. I wonder—how can we possibly buy Mrs. Gridley's house without being ghouls?"

That was a puzzler. We asked Daisy Haven.

"Why, you aren't ghouls at all!" she said, settling us temporarily in a hut she'd found in Carmel Woods. "You wouldn't want Gert Gridley's home unless she wanted to move. Now would you? No. I asked her the other day if she wasn't tired of polishing furniture and she said she *adores* it. She's especially happy right now. Her nephew and his family are coming from Kentucky to spend Thanksgiving. Gert worships her relatives, you know, and she's very hospitable. Now, then! Let's go exploring in the valley. Wouldn't you like a ranch?"

On the way back after inspecting two-acre ranches too near the river, I heard myself say: "All right. One more talk with Mrs. Gridley and we'll forget it."

"She's already said *no*," Ruth reminded me. "What else is there to talk about?" Her glance was like a cash report.

"The point is this—" and here was recently acquired wisdom—"when a price has been mentioned—even if it's high—the idea of selling gets into the air. Ideas have power."

"Let's take one thing at a time." Daisy turned to Ruth. "There are *lovely* houses on my list, but your husband will never appreciate them until you've put the Gridley place out of your mind." This was separation of the sexes—the next house would have a spectacular kitchen, and they'd be girls together. "I'll make an appointment with Gert and we'll get it over with."

Mrs. Gridley couldn't see us until Monday. Her voice on the phone had shot up an octave. Thanksgiving was turning into a family reunion with other relatives arriving from San Francisco. The Kentucky people had brought two small children and a collie pup.

"Now, then," said Daisy, again addressing Ruth as she hung up, "the next house I want to show you has a charming kitchen which is called a keeping room—"

"I think," Ruthie mused, "we'd better wait until Monday, don't you? What time in our appointment?"

"Eleven o'clock." They exchanged a glance of communication. "Yes, there *is* that about living in Carmel," said Daisy, wisely. "People with too many extra bedrooms must be prepared to entertain house guests, ready or not."

That was the key. That weekend the teething collie pup who shredded the plastic webbing in Mrs. Gridley's sun chaise in the patio and knocked over her azalea pots and dug a cave near the steps was a factor in what happened later, but he was entirely coincidental. The Kentucky Gridleys bought him en route and on impulse, which was also coincidental. So was the fact that they were young parents raising two small fry in a permissive fashion; the boys, when released on the public, were appalling. The arrival of the other San Francisco relatives who had driven down because the weather was fine probably would have occurred in the normal course of events. And the unexpected appearance of a highly emotional old friend who had just spent six weeks in Reno—and couldn't find a vacant room anywhere in Carmel—was the sort of thing that happens to everybody.

What impressed me when I thought it all over was this: eleven o'clock on that Monday morning was perfect timing. And what led us to *that?*

We knocked. We waited. There was a scratchy movement in the hall, and then Mrs. Gridley appeared at the open front door. She was in bathrobe, apron and woolly slippers with her hair in a ponytail. She'd *had* it. The house was a mess, she said, and she wouldn't think of letting anybody in. But she needed sympathy and lingered in the doorway.

This had been her first encounter with her grandnephews from Kentucky, and the next meeting would be too soon. They were already a menace to society. What were parents thinking of these days?

"Well, darling!" said Daisy. "I've said all along that you ought to buy a charming, one-bedroom cottage and use it as a *base*. Dear, you should travel around on those lovely new freighters the way the other girls do."

"I wish I were on a world cruise right this second!" cried Mrs. Gridley. "I'd rather be in Moscow than to have to straighten up this house!"

A bell rang somewhere in my head, and I stepped into the ring.

"Mrs. Gridley," I said, "I will give you thus-and-so for the property."

She was insulted. It was a thousand dollars less than we'd got for ours and five thousand less than the house was worth.

"Why, I wouldn't *think* of it! I wouldn't take a cent less than so-and-so!" she cried.

I countered. She countered. We went into the waltz. My auditor held her breath.

"Oh, all *right,*" Mrs. Gridley said finally. *"Sold!* Oh, Daisy—look at my sun chaise. Look what that damn dog did to my lovely plants!"

Thus it came about—we bought a house that wasn't for sale with money from a house that couldn't be sold, and everybody was happy. Mrs. Gridley disposed of heirlooms to other Gridleys, bought a charming one-bedroom cottage down the street, locked it up and went off on a freighter trip with some of the girls.

We moved in, and it was a small miracle—step number seven.

And here we are at step number eight:

Metaphysical journals have printed testimonials of healing for three quarters of a century or more. Many lack proof because only the writer of the testimony can know for sure what happened; but time and again I'd read these words: *"I was healed of smoking!"* and found in, under and around the words an honest and joyful note of surprise.

One night shortly after we had moved into the new house, I had an experience which brought the whir of angel feathers. In an attack of coughing my breathing pattern went out of rhythm and my lungs continued to expel air long past the point where a new supply was essential. Sharp whacks between the shoulder blades revived me. When I could move again, I hurled a half pack of filtered flip-top coffin nails across the room.

"Last cigarette again?" wondered Ruthie.

"This time," I said, "I'm going to *study*." Like Sagebrush Sam, I decided to speak my Word.

Step number nine:

There was, at least, the novelty of new approach. Snapping the lighter and filling up the ash trays, I nevertheless began some disciplined reading, nothing but metaphysics—Troward, Holmes, Maurice Nicoll, Ouspensky, Bucke and the mystics. For reasons personal to me which needn't be discussed here, Pico della Mirandola's *Oration on the*

Dignity of Man lifted some hampering misconceptions. Here, *in the fifteenth century,* sometime in 1487, a young man was saying: "We have longed for that holy peace, that indivisible union, that seamless friendship through which all souls will not only be at one in that one mind which is above every other mind, but, in a manner which passes expression, will really be one in the most profound depths of being."

The search turned up some notable minds and aroused a lively new interest. And this was step number ten—the true beginning of a new and more affirmative approach to problems.

And then the Coincidence:

A program arranged long before took me to the Civic Auditorium in Oakland during a writers' week convention. In a panel discussion, also arranged long before, I noticed a colleague, who was also a student of metaphysics, wasn't smoking. Like so many creative people, she had made her own contributions to the economy of Durham, North Carolina, over a long period of years. I watched her like a hawk. Serene. No withdrawal symptoms. When had *this* happened?

It had happened at Easter, she said, or shortly thereafter. There had been no struggle whatever when she got right down to it. She'd had faith to begin with. Perhaps that speeded things along.

We drove back to the Monterey Peninsula together in my car, and she traced it back for me:

"First," she said, "don't try to quit. You don't want to be bothered thinking about cigarettes."

That struck me as a heartening approach.

She had attended Ernest Holmes' Easter service at the

Beverly theater. She had wanted to stop smoking for a long time but hadn't decided how to go about it. A remark of Ernest's during his lecture had given her the key. He had said: "The subjective mind is compelled to accept. By its very nature it *must* accept—and what, right now, are you asking it to do?"

I could believe this, of course; I *knew* it worked.

"But what about the lifetime habits, mannerisms, reflexes—they're all part of it."

"You treat to have the whole thing removed from your experience. I'll help if you like."

And then, unknowingly, I took step number eleven: "I really wish you would."

I asked for help, was grateful for it, and meant it.

A few evenings later, in my well-marked textbook, I found another passage to underline. It was important to me and it's to be found on page 222 of *Science of Mind.* Ernest Holmes was discussing the liquor habit, but his approach to the problem served me equally as well in working my way toward that last cigarette.

He wrote:

> A habit is a desire objectified . . . desire for some thing that will give satisfaction. At the root of all habit is one basic thing: *the desire to express life.* . . . Some express themselves constructively and some destructively. Suppose a man who has the liquor habit comes to you to be healed. You would not treat that *habit.* You would not pray for the man to be healed. You would know that you are dealing with a man who has the desire to express life and who, for the moment, thinks that he must express it in terms of intoxication. He once thought this expressed reality to him. He now knows that it does not, but he cannot with mere

will power stop it, for the habit appears to have taken complete possession of him. (We might well remember always that unless we control thought, it will control us.)

In giving treatment, first recognize who and what this man is, saying something like this: "This man is the full and complete expression of Truth, and as such he is free from any sense of limitation. . . . He has no longing outside of the longing to express his own divinity, and he has the assurance that he will be able to gratify this: 'Blessed are they who do hunger and thirst after righteousness (right living), for they shall be filled.' This thing which calls itself the liquor habit has no power over him and cannot operate through him. By the power of this word, which I am now speaking, this habit is completely and forever obliterated." Then mentally see him free and harmoniously expressing life and happiness.

What about that! *See him free.* A technique.

As my interest in study increased, I was certainly smoking less, but I tried not to think about it. The same nightly techniques which had been used in my work now were useful here. Directions given to the subjective mind should be cogent, polite, carefully phrased, Mary Austin said. I would think as I turned off the reading light: "There will be removed from my experience the reflexes, mannerisms and desires that were a part of my routine activity; I am moving now into another area of consciousness and so let it be."

One morning at three o'clock I reached across for the filter-tips and stopped. Five minutes must have ticked away until I found a phrase to describe what I was trying to do. Before long I drifted back to sleep, and when I awakened in the morning, the words *habit surgery* were still in my mind.

There was a professional development out of which came step number twelve. Pressure mounted as we prepared to tape the summer shows in advance; this meant doubling up on the scripts—the current deadlines to be met while writing the summer scripts in advance. No social life. No interruptions. The locked gate. The shut-off phone. *Work.* The summer story that year was amusing, and I enjoyed doing it. When the last script had been mailed, Ruth and I started south in the car to attend the recording sessions.

We had reached the Hollywood Freeway and the old familiar tension prompted me to say:

"Ruthie? Got a cigarette?"

She always has a cigarette. She smokes Black Cats, a Canadian brand. They are difficult to find in this country. We go to Canada every two or three years to visit Dot and Bruce Hutchison and always bring back a supply.

Ruth handed me a Black Cat, reached across, pushed the car lighter, and said, casually:

"That must be your first cigarette in several weeks."

Several weeks!

The glowing lighter was lifted, but I declined it. She put it back. When had I smoked that last one—that final cigarette? I didn't know. And where was my beloved lighter? What about the big desk ashtray which a ceramist friend had made for me? The lighter, Ruth said, was in the top drawer of the desk in the living room; and a couple of weeks ago she had noticed that a boxful of paper clips had been emptied into the ashtray on my desk.

I handed back the Black Cat. She smoked it. And it didn't hurt her. She smokes only three or four times a week. And she doesn't inhale.

"I must remind myself to smoke more," she had said once upon a time. "I think it helps to keep my weight down."

I drove along toward Hollywood without fear of the speeding zombies, in exultation—it actually had happened and I was free.

10

For Saint, Sinner or Sagebrush Sam

Harlan Ware tossed the yellow pages of manuscript on my desk. "There it is, Bill. Habit surgery. To the best of my memory, those were the steps." He added: "But only *I* will know that it really happened."

True. The pattern is forever the same: to be healed of illness, of grief, of lack or limitation, or of habit, the process begins within. With consent. With belief. With what Ernest Holmes called an already-believing attitude of mind. Testimonials make interesting reading but, in the end, only the open-minded who seek—and discover—can know without doubt that a Law is available which responds impersonally, impartially, to saint, sinner or Sagebrush Sam.

Somebody, by taking thought, removes an invisible barrier, steps into a new area of consciousness—and a healing has taken place. How simple it seems when stated thusly! *Healing is the discovery of the Divinity Within.* What could be a more individual experience? And yet, once discovered, it leads to the awareness of a universal Law.

Awareness is the key word.

For example: two little girls seeking shells set out with their gaily decorated pails along a sandy beach one summer day. They were gone an hour. One returned in triumph with all she could carry. The other came back with wet shoes, sand in her hair and an empty bucket. She reported that there *were* no shells.

Same beach. Same abundance. But there had been a different quality of awareness.

One child had faith before; she has conviction now.

The other, with the weary wisdom of the sophisticate, reports a universe woefully lacking in seashells. And she's absolutely right—in her use of awareness. She can prove it, too: her pail is empty and her feet are wet.

Affirmative faith isn't easy to come by for many of us. In some cases we take a battering before the search even begins.

Two young college girls of our acquaintance insisted upon touring Europe in a fast, low-cost, all-expense guided bus trip. The beguiling brochure, picturing lazy days and languid, happy tourists lingering on the Lido offered: ALL OF EUROPE IN SEVENTEEN DAYS. "You can tell your friends you've been there!" The girls promised to write often but as it turned out, there was time for only one postcard. The bus stopped at Innsbruck just long enough for them to buy a stamp. They wrote:

"There's gotta be a better way!"

Many battered tourists on this planet ready to seek a better way have turned to metaphysics only to be discouraged by glib testimonials of instant healings attested to in tortured language—the near-meaningless metaphysical clichés, the upside-down words frozen into form like bugs in amber. For those who are searching—yes; there have been and will continue to be instant healings. But an honest account calls for the report of long, slow ones, too. And the outright failures.

In a seminar lecture, Ernest Holmes said:

"Too many practitioners say: 'I only give one treatment.' I often called their bluff in past years because I used to be much meaner than I am now. I would say to them: 'All right, I have a man I've been working with for nine months and I think he's a little worse. You just come and speak the word.' There were no takers."

The stubborn cases, the failures, the incidents in which the student refuses to give his consent to being healed (there are those who enjoy their misery, or are bored, or tired, and who want to "die out of it") are given no publicity when not actually hushed up.

In the past seventy-five years, thousands of metaphysical healings have been reported, enough to invite investigation on the part of reasonable people who have bounced around long enough to decide there's "gotta be a better way." But the study calls for dedication, and patience, and an open mind. The healing detailed in the preceding chapter came swiftly—after years of study. To maintain an affirmative attitude against the assault of the negative daily headlines and news announcements, the impact of the heedless and agnostic personalities, the daily waking nightmare of an indifferent and unbelieving world, is anything but easy—but learning how to translate the fevered scene into a longer view is magnificently rewarding.

"In the silence of your own consciousness, alone with the great Reality," Ernest said, in the lecture just quoted, ". . . see whether you have true love and forgiveness and more conviction to bring to bear, not to influence the Law, *but to be operated upon by the Law* with a mathematical and mechanical certainty at the level of your conviction."

The words "true love and forgiveness" often occurred in the lectures, and we are beginning to understand how compassion and forgiveness can heal.

One Wednesday evening last spring in Founder's Church, during the weekly study session which is called "the meeting of the sixteen hundred friends," a startling incident occurred.

We believe there is a healing consciousness of great power present in that sanctuary when large numbers of convinced students and metaphysicians meet for meditation and study. Sometimes we see immediate results. We did that night.

In a talk on "forgiveness" I ad-libbed a passage which, when reviewed later, seemed in no way remarkable. "Do not hold resentment," I said, in effect. "Or bitterness. For your own sake, if no other, love and forgive."

Somewhere far back in the sanctuary a woman sobbed. Those close to her were aware of hushed whispers and a stirring as I went on with my discourse.

Later, when saying good night to the sixteen hundred friends in the foyer, an elderly gentlewoman pushed her way eagerly toward me through the throng. "Dr. Hornaday!" She held her right hand high above her head, opening and closing her fingers. "I want you to know I've been healed. My first visit here—and I've been healed!" Her face was wet with tears, the glow of excitement unmistakably genuine.

She had never read a metaphysical book in her life and

had come to the meeting only because she was desperate. A friend had insisted that joining a study group certainly couldn't do her any harm. During her years of suffering, diagnosed as a painful form of arthritis, the fingers of her right hand had gradually closed into a fist.

Whatever was said about "forgiveness" stirred a darkened corner of her mind, and she realized with elation that she actually had forgiven someone for an injury over which she had brooded bitterly in earlier years.

"This is now, a new moment, the past is forever gone—" I had said.

A tingling startled her; she found her heart lifting in sudden warmth, accompanied by an already believing awareness, not of being gradually healed, but of having been healed in an instant just past! Her fingers unlocked slightly. She began to direct them to open, and all the while was congratulating herself on having so long ago forgiven; why, she'd carried with her only a faint memory of an old resentment!

In recognizing this, had she freed herself of self-inflicted pain? I do not know. Doctors wouldn't know. Psychiatrists wouldn't know. All would have opinions. Not even the person healed would know what actually had happened; and only she would know with certainty that whereas she had been desperate, now she was healed.

She told me about it over coffee, which is served to the sixteen hundred friends after the lecture. She had lost faith in religion years ago, she said, and now added wistfully: "I wish someone would tell me how to *imagine* God."

The mystics, Dr. Holmes told his audience at the Beverly one Sunday, described God as Love, Truth, Beauty and Wisdom.

"Certainly God is in all four," he had said, "the Invisible Presence in Love, Truth, Beauty and Wisdom. Whatever is true is God, whether we can understand it or not. Whatever is beautiful and wise and loving is God."

I walked out to the parking lot with friends who had witnessed the demonstration.

We walked around a pile of lumber which had been unloaded that afternoon for work in the new chapel.

"While the sanctuary was being built," someone said, "I often saw Dr. Holmes during the noon hour when I peeked through the fence—to bless the work, you know. Dr. Holmes would be sitting on a pile of lumber talking to the workmen. They always seemed so animated. Were they discussing philosophy, d'you suppose?"

"Ernest did a lot of listening," I told them. "The workmen fascinated him. And it was mutual."

There was autumn nostalgia in the memory and, driving home that evening, I could all but see Ernest as a sidewalk superintendent not content to watch through the peepholes in the fence but, whenever there was time, impelled to join the workmen. The architect had translated the idea—a building symbolizing the Allness of God—into sketches, blueprints and then into bricks and mortar; for Ernest here was a lifetime of thought taking tangible form!

At noon he would pick his way around mounds of debris and join any group—hod carriers, plasterers, electricians, plumbers—as if he expected a warm welcome, and always got it. "I'm Ernest Holmes." Often they were surprised to find so eminent a man so easy to know. Soon it was, "Hi, Doctor—sit down!" One thing about him puzzled them. He still spoke stiffly of the "edifice." They openly called it a "church."

He was interested in them, in their work, their lives, what they read, what they thought, and how they felt about theology. His stories often rocked them with laughter. I wish we had a snapshot of him sitting there with the workmen and their lunchboxes in the slant of the fall sunlight.

When Emerson's "heaven and earth for beams and rafters" had been translated into small overhead circles of light in the graceful gray arch of the sanctuary, and the "edifice" had become a reality, he said:

"The only question we need ask ourselves is this: Do we in our thought, attitude, the way we live, bear witness to the living truth that God is all there is? Do we, in this sanctuary and in our lives, hold to Love, Truth, Beauty and Wisdom? Make that a policy. That's all the creed you'll ever need."

And then shortly after the more than sixteen hundred comfortable theater seats had been installed in the sanctuary, he stopped calling the building an "edifice." Soon he was spending hours there in meditation. After the organ had been installed—and it did become the Hazel Holmes Memorial Organ—he remarked one day: "I went over to the church for a while this morning and . . ." That was the end of the tiptoe semantics, though I still walked gingerly around "Mortgage"—even though the Wiltern congregation, the Board of Trustees and generous friends had taken most of the concern out of the word.

And now, if he could only know, this last Easter morning we spoke to thousands at a hilltop Sunrise Service, and nine thousand or more in our three services at Founder's Church, including the overflow in the new chapel, where they watched the services on closed-circuit television; perhaps we didn't keep the service as simple as he would have liked—starkly simple, with blackboard and double-breasted blue suit, and no flowers and no choir: that was *his* idea of a tiptop Easter service! But we were true to his creed in other particulars: there was Love, Truth, Beauty and—we trust—Wisdom in the services.

For his first sermon in Founder's Church, Dr. Holmes was at his shining best. Nobody had to beg him to put on his black shoes—all the things Hazel once urged upon him he now performed in grave, silent obedience.

He stood behind the pulpit and let the language soar; stood on a three-inch step because the rostrum was too tall. He enjoyed having those extra inches and said so and got the kind of laugh which used to explode in the theater. The congregation faced the choir loft, behind which we now have the great mural, an idea of Ernest's: the Allness of God expressed in symbols of man's search for Truth, with the Lamp of Knowledge at the base.

Ernest couldn't sing. Not a note. It was embarrassing when he tried. Hazel once said: "Papa, don't attempt it—just *breathe*." But he early came to admire the choir. There were superior voices among the eighty-five gifted singers, and he stood below them, moving his lips soundlessly, looking serene, and musical and ministerial.

Ministerial? Only on Sunday. And, of course, on the formal occasions such as christenings, though it was startling sometimes when the beauty of the children overwhelmed him and he needed his handkerchief. There was no subtlety in his reach for it. He would pull up the robe, dig into his hip pocket—and blow.

For several weeks I deluded myself into thinking that the building of Founder's Church had reawakened his interest in creative work. I was wrong. He would detach himself even during discussions, then grow aware of his own silence and wave the question aside. "You handle it, Bill."

In 1958 we had published the jointly written book, *Help for Today,* which later came to be used as a textbook in study groups for beginning students of metaphysics in many churches. I wanted us to do a series of such books in which case histories would dramatize the teaching, thus making abstract ideas easier for the uninitiated to understand. After Hazel left, his interest began to languish and one day, speaking of a healing which had dramatic overtones, I said: "There's a chapter for our next book, Ernest."

"Your next book," he said abruptly.

We were in my new office. He had declined to have an office of his own in the church, but he often wandered into mine, sat off to one side, listened to whatever was going on and offered opinion only when it was asked of him.

A fine spray of water washed over the ferns in the meditation garden, and now he stood in the doorway watching the drip from the leaves while I answered a phone call. He realized how abruptly he had spoken. When I put the receiver down, he came back.

"Hazel and Prince will be waiting for me someday," he said, taking a nearby armchair. "I don't know where or how, or in what unimaginable next dimension, but I've always known that the loves of your life can't be lost, here or hereafter." He sat with his elbows on the arms, shoulders hunched, his blue-eyed gaze far beyond the walls. "No marriage could have been richer than ours, you know. And Prince taught me more about consciousness and love than I learned from many professors. The other night in a dream I heard that peculiar little bark of his, a singular, special greeting, just for me, his way of saying, 'Here's Ernest!' I'll hear that again in some other reality."

There was a long pause. I didn't break it and at last he said:

"One day Prince and I were in the garden watching a caterpillar. The caterpillar was in our world yet in his own dimension, inching along, his mind preoccupied with caterpillar worries, whatever they may be. I knew something about his future, however, and in the long view he was in better shape than he suspected. Some instinct would take him out of the cold weather and into a cocoon, into a kind of death, in warm darkness; and what then?—one glorious spring morning he'd find himself with a wider view—the same world seen from another level. He'd take it for granted, of course, but he'd be a butterfly soaring over a sunlit garden. If a law does this for an insect, what d'you suppose it does for the higher consciousness of man? I can't help being *curious* about it, Bill. It's sure to be an improvement. I've always known that. I was born knowing it."

This conversation puzzled and concerned me. What was he up to?—the mentor who had caught me up sharply whenever, in the stress of our complex activities, I'd given away to a moment's doubt, or had allowed the negatives to creep in? What was he giving his own consent to?

One afternoon we were scheduled to speak at the dedication of a suburban church. He rarely drove his own car now, so I called for him at the new house, a sort of tudor mansion, on Lorraine Boulevard. He greeted me abstractedly and was silent the whole way.

He'd had an illness in the summer. Not at all a serious illness, but his attitude had concerned us because he spoke of joining Hazel as casually as if he were planning a journey abroad, a man with an interesting itinerary—"It'll be a fine trip, wish you could join me!"—was his attitude. He was *not* taking a negative view, he protested; he was a tourist trying to restrain his curiosity: what existed beyond the mountain range, the countryside which brought from mystics the same report, while the psychics all came back with different stories? Other dimensions! What unimaginable wonders would there be?

I'd not been sure he wasn't disappointed when he recovered so quickly; but in his remarkable ad-lib talk at the dedication ceremony that afternoon he heartened me when he said:

"It's possible for anybody to forget the way; it doesn't matter how much he knows. I forgot a while back and got kind of sick, but now I'm remembering again and getting well again. It's possible for anybody to block the channels through which the Living Presence expresses Itself."

And it was possible, as he often said, for the student to withhold consent to his own recovery, to accept what he took for the ultimate escape, and to "die out of it." Or, as in his own case, to decide to move on. Once during the illness he had said to me:

"When that big day comes, you'll say a few words, of course—but keep 'em *few,* Bill. Play the organ loudly and give the people my regrets. I won't be there. Just say that I can't attend the ceremony because I'll be busy elsewhere."

But now as he faced the friendly suburban congregation which had crowded into a lovely new church designed to express Light and Life, his voice took on the old enthusiasm:

"We are the first group of people who ever formulated a religion, code of ethics, tenets of belief, that has no personal opinion in it, no personal preference to it; that has no one to please, and no one to displease. *All,* we know, *is within.* I believe that Science of Mind is the answer of the ages to the call of the ages. I believe it is a thing of destiny, and I believe it will extend around the world, and heal the world. I do not know when." He paraphrased Browning: " 'I shall arrive; sometime; somehow; some day; in God's good time, I shall arrive.' We offer not a distant event, it is here; it is now; it is today.

"Let this be a lesson to the world that others seeing this light shall find the way again, there in the night. And never forget this, one man with God is a totality, is a completeness. One opinion consistent with the truth is not a positive statement but an absolute fact with no relativity in it at all. Our time should be devoted to knowing that Truth which will set men free from the problems of ignorance, that Truth which alone can bring enlightenment to the world, that war should cease, that people should live together as harmonious human beings who have recognized the Divinity in each other. We have lighted a torch, and the flame comes from a wick which is rooted in the mind of God.

"Let us bear witness in this edifice of light with its glass walls and gardens to the concept that God is Love, Truth, Wisdom and Beauty; more—we bear witness to that which is beyond beauty, the essence of Beauty. To that which is beyond knowledge, to the essence of Wisdom. To that which is beyond love and living, to the essence of Love and Life."

He walked briskly to the car. My heart lifted as we drove away. Now, in the wake of a successful speech, perhaps I could arouse his interest in our book, work with him at his own house in the evenings, and we'd get back to laughter and the creative obsession once again. He was at his best when functioning and under pressure of deadlines. I'd been saving a good evidential. I told it now and expected a warm reaction.

Philip Prior, who had written the check for that six thousand dollars after my second Sunday at the Belmont, offered to attest to a remarkable demonstration. Early in his study of Science of Mind he had turned to Ernest's textbook for guidance and had quickly grasped the techniques. Being himself an engineer working in electronics, he accepted Ernest's blunt statement: *"Unless there were a method for spiritual mind practice, then such practice would not be scientific. Unless there were a definite technique, its use could not be taught."* Philip Prior understood that the practice called for something beyond the mere use of the subjective mind; he saw at once that the metaphysician in approaching his problem, whatever it was, adjusts to a greater reality.

The problem then bedeviling him was a professional one—the need for invention in a field in which he was pioneering. There were no charts—it called for originality—more, for genius. Every spare moment away from his office had been spent in study of metaphysics. He sensed that here he would find a way to a fuller realization of his own talents.

One evening he went peacefully to sleep, and it was as if in his dreams he had experienced an expansion of consciousness. Something carried him beyond an invisible barrier, and he lost all sense of limitation. Some time during the night he dreamt of a blueprint which detailed an astonishing new approach to his problem. In the morning when he awakened, the dream had faded. There was a memory of having looked around sleepily for paper and pencil—but that was the only remnant of what now began to seem unreal. By breakfast time he knew only that he had dreamt; he deplored the lack of a pencil and pad beside the bed. Mrs. Prior assured him there *had* been a pencil between the leaves of a novel she'd been reading; too bad it hadn't been where he could find it.

That night when he retired he found not only a pad and pencil on the bed table, but his wife's novel open to the flyleaf—*on which was sketched the details of the blueprint he had seen in his dream!* He had done this when half asleep, and now the priceless details were there before him and in readable form.

The incident led to the establishment of his own company, the foundation of his fortune.

I told the story to Ernest as we sped toward town.

It brought only a long pause.

"Bill," he said carefully at last, "you know we'll not write that book. You'll write it, yourself—but not I."

"But when, Ernest? I haven't time to write a book alone. Two sermons on Sunday, another on Wednesday, five radio talks each week, weddings, christenings, the office routine—"

"You're the fella who wanted a church!" he said sharply. But then he half turned and put a hand on my shoulder: "*Treat* for somebody to help—the way I did when I needed an assistant. Somebody, a writer, will come along who thinks as we do, and wants to get some of it down.

"Bill, I'm serious about this," he said, as we turned into Lorraine and approached his house. "I'm fine now, but it won't be long. I know this planet as well as I want to. I don't plan to come this way again."

He thanked me gravely for the chauffeuring and the compliments and I watched him go up the walk. In other years Prince, the German shepherd, would have come racing out to greet him, a bouncing, animate expression of love and welcome. In other years Hazel would hear them skylarking in the front hall. Appearing at the head of the stairs, she would call: "What particular rarity today, Papa?"

I felt his loneliness as he took out his key, unlocked the door and went in. As always, he hadn't looked back. The door closed.

11

A Recipe for Living

> Through spiritual discernment, we see that we have within us a Power which can overcome every obstacle in our experience and set us safe, satisfied and at peace, healed and prosperous in a new light and a new life.
>
> —ERNEST HOLMES

The healing Power within us is equally responsive whether we light a candle or a joss stick, worship in mosque, shrine, temple, church or on the highest hill. It will not forsake us if we doubt Its existence, forget to perform certain religious rituals, or if we are immersed in the guilt of past mistakes. Nor will it do us any special favors because of our politics or the color of our skin. It is forever impersonal as Law.

But it is personal as the Presence; and it is Love. It will respond to recognition and identification in our daily living:

It responds to affirmative prayer.

Sally Steen Kincey knew this, forgot it for a while, but remembered it again. We are using real names in this account and another to follow because both are stories of professional people whose identification with the Ernest Holmes philosophy is of public record and neither is reluctant to have the story told. In Sally Kincey's case, study of the Science of Mind was a lifetime affair. Her uncle, Reverend J. Arthur Twyne, had been the first Negro minister to be given a charter for a church of Religious Science, the third church of Religious Science to be organized. Sally, christened Saphronia, attended Sunday school and was brought up, to use Dr. Holmes' phrase, "in faith, not fear." And what we learn in childhood is never really forgotten.

Dr. Holmes was an important figure to her from the beginning. He understood her ambition to become a dancer. There was always a kindly, joking exchange when they met; she was a leggy youngster who could leap into an *arabesque* and put a sparkle of humor in it. "A girl with a future," he told Uncle Arthur. Ambitious young people cherish such remarks.

There were family legends about Dr. Holmes. Once at a convention he took the baby away from Mrs. Twyne and wouldn't give him up. He carried young Arthur, Jr., all around the hotel, inside and out, showing him to everybody, including total strangers. Arthur was about a year old then, starchy and bright-eyed under his white bonnet. "Have you ever seen a more beautiful baby in your life?" he'd ask, and his eyes were misty. A very sentimental man, Dr. Holmes.

But not always. Sally never forgot how he had impressed a Sunday audience. Somebody had complained that too many non-Caucasians were attending the services. The people who were in the theater that day still remember his remarks.

Dr. Holmes took his place at the rostrum and waited—soon you could hear a pin drop. Still he waited. It was a standing-room-only crowd. Not even the standees whispered or moved. At last he spoke:

"I have been told that too many non-Caucasians attend these lectures. True, there are Caucasians and non-Caucasians in this congregation. But this we must affirm: we are all children of One Living God—One Life that permeates all, without exception—One Intelligence that governs all—and, most important, every man and woman who abides in the universe is a significant identity in the One Universal Consciousness. Our doors will forever be open to all. Whoever you are, be proud—you are a Divine Idea in the Mind of God."

Everybody applauded.

That took care of that.

He continued his lecture, satisfied that the matter had been settled once and for all. He would never refer to it again.

Uncle Arthur told Sally to go to the lectures whenever she could because Dr. Holmes was a great man and she wouldn't see his like again. After she outgrew Sunday school, she regularly made the long bus trip to the theater where he spoke on Sunday morning. Often the lecture was over her head. Indeed, sometimes Dr. Holmes himself seemed to be as baffled as she was.

"What an amazing statement!" he remarked one time, putting down his chalk, as if just hearing what he himself had said. "I wonder what I meant? Does anybody know?"

Nobody did.

"Well, let's remember it," he suggested gravely. "If one of us should figure it out, we'll all take a step ahead."

At such times Sally didn't know whether he was joking or if, perhaps, a tremendous idea had come from inner space because he'd got himself out of the way. Uncle Arthur often quoted Emerson, who recommended getting our own "bloated nothingness" out of the way—a suggestion so lacking in ego points that not too many people tried it.

In those days Sally had a pretty clear idea of the meaning of consciousness. Some of it she had heard, and some she'd worked out for herself.

In the beginning white children do not know they are white, and Negro children do not know they are Negroes. Each is an individual area of awareness locked in an individual mind; both look out upon the world with the same kind of vision and discover, presumably, the same general countryside. A lilac is a lilac, an orchid an orchid, and both are manifestations of God, and so are we. The pigment of our skin has nothing to do with consciousness.

On this planet there seems to be *quantity* and *quality* of consciousness and varying degrees of sensitivity in individuals; but there's little question, at this point, that whoever we are, we have within us the potential for more awareness than we're likely to experience. We aren't half trying.

But sometimes an expansion of consciousness comes as a gift. Sally overheard something once that changed her life forever. Names and details are lost in the mists of childhood, but this was the way of it.

The children were clustered around somebody's front

porch after church, the girls in their hats and gloves and shiny shoes, and the boys in suits and neckties. An important man had come home with the adults. He'd stopped in for coffee. He was an actor. He wore starched French cuffs and golden cuff links and at church everybody had treated him with deference. The children crowded into the house uninvited and made themselves small in the corners. Young Sally never forgot what he said:

"Show business offers opportunities our youngsters mightn't find elsewhere, except, of course, in sports," he observed, after making gracious remarks about the homemade cake. "If a child is disciplined and prepared and has enough talent—and is lucky enough to be in the right place at the right time—he has as much chance as anyone. Eventually, with real ability, the doors open, and something happens. Any of you ever hear of Bert Williams?"

The adults said: "Of course."

"Bert Williams was a Negro entertainer born to have his name in lights," the man told the children. "When you saw him on the stage in the spotlight, each slight move of his white-gloved fingers meant something special; there was humor and sadness in his every move and in his voice. Somehow he got into instant communication with an audience—nobody ever could figure out how it was done. It was genius. He appeared in the Ziegfeld Follies, and in two-a-day vaudeville—he was famous in the big cities long ago. Alone upstage, in his frock coat, with the white gloves, and with the spotlight centered on him, he would just stand there and *think*, and pretty soon people would begin to laugh and applaud. What *was* that? Who could possibly know? He told his stories to the most fashionable audiences in the world, and it was always the same. At the sight of him the house hushed. With perfect timing, creating the mood and suiting himself to it, he'd sort of chant an anecdote in his deep, sad voice, and there would be both heartbreak and humor all around him—and afterward a storm of applause. Night after night throughout his career he stopped the show.

"But d'you know what would happen later in the evening after his tremendous triumph? He and the other stars, like Mr. Eddie Cantor, would leave by the stage door and duck across the street to the hotel. Mr. Cantor and the rest would go in the front way. They were white. Mr. Williams, who was a genius, but a Negro, would go down the alley. While Mr. Cantor and his friends were riding up the front elevator in the hotel, Mr. Williams would take the service elevator to the same floor. Then they'd meet in the corridor and go into Mr. Cantor's room or Mr. Williams' room and play cards. The white men were apologetic about this, but that's the way things were. Because Mr. Williams was a famous star, the theatrical hotels let him have a room for the run of the play, even though it was against the custom. It was understood he'd try to keep out of sight of the guests who might object to having a Negro living in the same hotel. Don't think I'm bitter, children. I'm telling you the way it is. But here's my point—now listen: you yourself can be so big, so enormous inside, and so warmhearted, and such a decent person, that such prejudice can't hurt you. You can rise above it.

"What did all that nonsense matter if Bert Williams could stand alone in the spotlight with his quiet songs and quiet conversation and make all those people love him for the evening, anyway—make them laugh or cry, depending on *his* mood, on what *he* felt! Wasn't that magnificent? You know it was. So if you have talent, work at it, work at it, *work* at it. You don't get anything the easy way. Nobody does."

The man went away after an hour or so. There's nobody around who remembers him now. But he left an idea. And an idea can change everything.

Arthur, Jr., was taking piano lessons. He probably practiced harder than most other small boys. Lavinia, his sister, studied harder than many other little girls. And Sally had decided to be a dancer and she danced all the time and never missed a lesson and kept the picture in her mind's eye day and night—the quiet Mr. Bert Williams alone in the spotlight with the audience hushed and waiting so they wouldn't miss a word or an expression or a movement of his fingers.

Arthur Twyne, Jr., became a professional pianist—the first Negro staff member at CBS in Hollywood. Lavinia became a teacher, the wife of a post-office executive, and a cultured and gracious lady.

And Sally became a dancer when she was very young.

Very young. She was a junior in Muir Technical High School in Pasadena when she heard about an opening for a dancer at the White Horse Tavern, a night club. Her mother wouldn't have approved, she knew, but then her mother worked nights as a chef and didn't get home until three o'clock in the morning. No need to worry the family until she'd landed the job! By that time she would have demonstrated not only that she was a talented dancer with a future but also that she could do her homework backstage. She could get established as a dancer before it was necessary to say too much about it around the house.

Early that evening Sally left an armload of books with a startled doorman and called on the manager of the White Horse Tavern, offering to show him a few routines. They went out to the dance floor. He watched cold-eyed. She hadn't quite finished the first number when he said: "You're hired, kid."

So she went to work for forty-five dollars a week.

A young musician who owned a jalopy drove her home each evening after the last performance. She would say good-by to him, slip into the house, still in make-up and spangles, and plunge into the shower. When her mother came home in the pre-dawn darkness after the eight-hour shift in the hotel kitchens, she would find studious, dependable Sally, the high-school junior, in sweet repose, completed homework on the bed table. A very satisfactory daughter, her mother often said—helped around the house, made her own clothes, was never tardy, and stayed in the dead center of her class at school. (She was bright enough to have earned higher grades, of course, but she spent every spare moment dancing.)

The career was launched. Mom didn't suspect, and all was well. They weren't even ships passing in the night. When Sally bolted away for Muir Tech in the morning, toast in hand, her mother was still sleeping, and when her mother came home, Sally was sleeping. They got together on Sundays. But it was the hotel's busy season and often Mom filled-in weekends or put in overtime. Of course, if Sally's conscience had bothered her she might have wakened her a bit early on a Saturday afternoon but, for one reason or another, this didn't seem practical.

It was a glorious period, just the way it was. She had been a success from opening night.

She knew how to handle all the problems on stage and off. It was as if she had been a professional dancer in another life. After the excitement of the first few performances she learned to concentrate away from the beat of jazz rhythm, resolutely wrote her themes and kept up with the school assignments. Her first pay check seemed enormous, and she saved every cent of it; the next check plus the first added up to more cash than she'd ever seen before. Then the manager gave her a brief solo number on the second Saturday night. It was a hit—she could hear the sweet sound of swelling applause and wondered if Bert Williams' heart had always ached when he heard it, and if he, too, responded with love for the audience which almost brought tears. There was such an upwelling of gratitude that she took a second bow and finally blew them kisses with both hands.

She was on her way.

At two o'clock that morning the young musician let her out at the front gate and drove off as usual. Sally ran in and was fumbling for the light switch when she heard someone breathing hard in the dark. The lights blazed on. It was Mom.

Here was a high-school junior in golden tights, with a golden tiara on her head, and a golden cape tossed over her slim shoulders, and with inch-long eyelashes, because she never took off her makeup until she got home. She had her schoolbooks with her, but under the circumstances they didn't look wholesome. She hastily put them down, explained everything and piled money on the living room table. Sally displayed the thousand-word theme she had written between shows backstage, and told how she left right after the show with a nice, tired boy who was never invited in.

Her mother wasn't impressed. There was the smell of oil of peppermint in the house. Mom had come home from work early with a splitting headache and the headache had become a migraine when she discovered Sally's bed not slept in.

Money—studying—none of it mattered. The *principle* of the thing was wrong!

"Your White Horse Tavern is no place for a young girl to do her homework," Mrs. Steen told the night club manager the next evening. "Sally is too young to work in a night club—it's even against the law." It turned out, of course, that Sally had fogged up her age.

The manager was distressed to learn that he'd endangered his license by hiring a minor.

He fired Sally at once. But he said he was sorry to see her go.

"You'll be proud someday," he told Mrs. Steen.

"I'm proud now," she responded firmly. "Sally's a good, bright girl. But she's going to finish high school and maybe go to college."

The manager walked out to the car with them. "I'll tell you something else," he said. "I wouldn't worry too much about college. Let her get started. She's star material."

And she was.

And she is now.

A young married woman with talent can find plenty of dancing jobs, and being married means that families can't interfere. Sally married the young musician immediately after graduation. They went off on a three-day honeymoon to a hotel near an amusement park and when that was over, they went looking for jobs. They were both too young and scatterwitted to realize the obligation they'd assumed. There were bitter spats, but they made up and both kept working. Sally's dancing was joyous and free: there was a glow about her. She had no trouble finding jobs. She would think of Mr. Bert Williams and the audience who applauded warmly and loved him. It was something to aim for—to be a female Bert Williams, think of that! A flash of humor in one's dancing brought an instant response, she found: that plus youth and grace and an inside feeling of gaiety, and a sense of being lithe and beautiful under the lights—why, you'd get that *already-believing* view of the future, and there was your name in lights! *Sally Steen.*

"You're doing all right, Sally," the manager said.

An overhead cable snapped during a performance at the Lincoln Theater on Central Avenue in Los Angeles. The first ominous cracking in the loft was followed by an echoing explosion. The heavy curtain drop tumbled down amid writhing lines and a billowing of velvet: a weight thudded heavily, and in the confusion it was discovered that Sally Steen lay unconscious on the stage.

She regained consciousness in the hospital. Lights, music, an applauding audience—then darkness—an endless nightmare. There were nurses and doctors and then a morning when she discovered that she couldn't move the fingers of her left hand, or her left arm, or her left leg. It took hours to get the idea through her head: the curtain drop had fallen on her; she was paralyzed on the left side.

Eleven months and twenty-three days later the doctors told her she would never walk again.

Uncle Arthur, her mother, members of the family, brought textbooks and metaphysical pamphlets, but she wasn't interested. Her young husband came to see her, apologized for the last spat, said he would stay married to her forever and carry her up and down stairs and push her wheel chair. She wanted none of that. It wasn't fair to him, and she couldn't abide pity. Mom knew a lawyer. . . .

The marriage was annulled.

"What good is a prayer of affirmation when you can't even move the little finger of your left hand?" Sally asked us recently when she told us the story of what has happened since. "What was the use of reading anything when the best doctors have told you that you'll never walk again? The nurses tried to take me to the physical therapy room, but I was too miserable to leave my bed. A nice young man, older—he was twenty-six—a theatrical manager—came to see me, to encourage me. He told me how great I would have been. That wasn't much help. It was all over for me, and I'd loved show business. For weeks I didn't want to live."

It's hard to find the proper get-well card for a paralyzed dancer. People sent her newspaper clippings, cartoons and jokes and theatrical news. She left them unread. One day a member of Uncle Arthur's church sent her a slim booklet which had been written for people who had a long way to go; it summed up thusly: Two men in Washington were paralyzed from the waist down. One was selling pencils on a street corner. The other was in the White House, President of the United States.

"It hit me very hard," Sally said. "It stirred old memories of Uncle Arthur's church and Sunday school."

She could remember the church on Vernon Avenue and the Sunday she got a glimmer of the great idea when the teacher said: "It isn't your mind, my mind, but God's Mind, and we can have as much of God Consciousness as we are able to understand." It was an overwhelming idea. It helped to explain Bert Williams, and how he could stand there and just *think* and the audience would respond; maybe he thought that he loved them in spite of all the problems, and that they loved him in spite of all the prejudices, and that everybody was together in a mysterious journey through a sad and funny world.

She had walked slowly home alone that day. On the way was a vacant lot with a few neglected orange trees on it, part of an old-time orchard. One of the trees had blossoms, and she decided to take a small branch home to put in water. But she didn't. A remarkable thing happened. A honey-bee invaded one of the blossoms. For the longest time she watched the bee and the flower. Was God's mind in the bee, too, and the flower? They seemed to be aware of each other and were important to each other, and she understood in a flash that she and the bee and the flower were very much related, all members of One Life, all part of the Mind of God. Understanding overwhelmed her for a moment, but then it faded and some of it was gone by the time she got home; but she had forever after a sense of the Oneness of all life and she kept the basic idea somewhere in her mind—up to the morning she woke up in the hospital and didn't care about anything because she couldn't move her leg.

But now the story of the man selling pencils on the

street corner and the other man in the White House illustrated what the teacher used to tell the class about the wonder of life. It was too often taken for granted because everybody was in headlong pursuit of something that in the end would tarnish and be left where thieves would break in and steal. She understood again: you could let your troubles blind you—cry, why did this have to happen to me, a dancer!—and then you'd never see the miracle. Or you could turn your mind to the *solution* and begin to see it and let it be revealed!

Dr. Holmes had spoken to the Sunday school class one Sunday—a great occasion in Uncle Arthur's church—an anniversary. Dr. Holmes said not to be discouraged if problems were sometimes difficult to solve. We didn't understand the principle well enough as yet to accomplish the kind of wonders Jesus achieved. But we were learning. We had, at least, part of the principle and we'd work and study and practice until we had it all, he said. There were problems which called for patience.

For an illustration he talked about an old hen sitting on her eggs. It took exactly twenty-one days to hatch little chicks. That was the Law. If the hen obeyed the Law and kept fertile eggs warm the proper length of time, chickens would hatch. You could see the Law at work under an old hen's feathers anytime you were so minded. He said, "Remember, when you have a good idea, stay with it until it hatches."

Sally began to daydream a little: if she couldn't be a dancer, she'd teach dancing. There was a way to do this. An Irish tap dancer, Johnny Boyle, had been desperately ill with silicosis, but he went right on teaching, and d'you know how? He designed tiny shoes to fit two fingers of his right hand, learned to use them as feet, and had taught himself to illustrate routines in this fashion; he had felt it necessary to do this because he knew more dance steps than anybody then alive, and he wanted to pass on everything he knew. He had worked in the coal mines of Pennsylvania in his boyhood—and his talent for dancing had helped him escape, and he was grateful.

A visitor from the theater had told her about Johnny Boyle one day, but she hadn't been attentive. Now the story came back into her mind. She was allowing herself to hope. Yet one must not ask the impossible. Johnny had been an expert and she had been a youngster starting her career; she would find practical dreams—perhaps she could become a set designer! That was it! She could study color, fabric and design from where she lay at this moment.

She rang for the nurse.

"Please take me to the therapy room," she said.

Multicolored hair ribbons which her mother had brought her, and which she had scorned to wear, were found in the drawer of the bed table. She selected the gayest of the lot and, while the nurse was tying it, fell to wondering: how would you tie a bow-knot in a hair ribbon with one hand when reaching back over your shoulder? Could it be done?

She decided to practice.

"You can be a star in the therapy room, you know," Sally said. "I don't mean a show-off. You can do all the hard things quietly, the way disciplined dancers do, and as soon as you begin to try, something inside says, 'Go ahead—it's worth it!' People often look grim and sweaty in a therapy room, so I wondered how it would be if I came in looking gay. I learned to put a ribbon in my hair with one hand and got some fun out of the challenge, and soon there were triumphs. The response I got was worth it. It isn't being hammy if you overcome obstacles and get the applause for it."

Before long Sally was exhibit A around the neighboring hospitals in Los Angeles. She is extraordinarily pretty—an intact, bright, colorful personality, warm, responsive and quick of wit. The therapists at Birmingham General Hospital in the Valley heard about her and one great day they sent an ambulance to take her there. Birmingham is a veterans' hospital and they asked her to demonstrate to Wacs and Waves what could be done with one hand. Soon she found herself making similar trips to Rancho Los Amigos or to the UCLA medical center. Before long she had made friends with doctors and therapists all over town. At Los Amigos she met a man named Jack Conway, an orthopedist, who followed her suggestions and created a light plastic cupped sling for her arm, the same color as her skin; and she now carried it comfortably, and usually unnoticed.

She was now starting each day with the textbook as she had done when she was a dancer. It helped with the day's discipline to study until breakfast, steadfastly. She would reject negatives and select affirmatives all day long. Many views are possible, but in a realistic, not Pollyanna way, bright ones can be as true as the grim ones in a world where nobody yet sees everything as it really is.

"Anybody who thinks that consistently using the Power of the Mind is easy hasn't tried it," Sally said. "Because you don't want to kid yourself. An idea has to be true or it won't work. You keep sorting things out to find the real truth. Then you select the idea you want to demonstrate and stay with it."

She began to improve in every way because she was affirmative and busy. Before long she could hop around, unafraid, without a crutch. Once when she was getting dressed to leave for Birmingham Hospital she felt a tingling in her left leg, beginning at the toes. Could it be true? She stood with both hands on the bureau, eyes closed and saw herself dancing, lithe and free, in an already-believing moment that would have her walking freely again. She feared the sensation might go away if she mentioned this to anyone, so she said: "Thank you, Father," to the Power within and rode to Birmingham the whole way, trying not to grin like an idiot.

"What're you so happy about?" the glum driver said.

"Well, for one thing, it's such a lovely day," Sally pointed out.

It was, too. He hadn't noticed.

What a miracle! The tingling was in her ankle now. She pictured herself walking, and then she tried to see herself dancing again—that was more difficult. She would dream about that at night.

One day a nurse said: "Sally! Didn't you just move your leg?"

She said, "I guess maybe I did!" And then, deliberately, moved it—it responded to orders!

The nurse ran for the doctors. They were astonished. They took more X rays. She could understand the X rays of the smashed shoulder herself, so that got pretty well fixed in her mind and she accepted it, but even the doctors said they couldn't understand what was happening to her leg.

Before long she was attending the rehabilitation school at Third and Broadway. Her knee began to respond and she could get up and down stairs now, one step at a time. She took an aptitude test, hoping that it would reveal a talent for set designing. Alas! It developed that she was in every way fitted to become a bookkeeper. So, heavyhearted but determined, she signed up for the course. The family needed money, and it was wrong to reject a talent; soon she had a daytime job, worked eight hours and studied bookkeeping five hours in the evening.

If she were not to be a set designer she could, at least, design colorful, tasteful clothes for herself—and did. She took to wearing pumps with high heels because they forced her to pick up her left foot and not drag it the easy way. She matched sling pumps and costumes and hair ribbons and tried to give a gay appearance, like a dancer off-stage, someone with *joie de vivre.*

She graduated and got a better job. Bookkeeping is not an exciting occupation for anyone who is at heart a dancer, but it pays well and, if you're good, there's always work to be had.

She was living at home again but making frequent trips to the hospital to show off her walking and her dexterity with her right hand. "I went into the wards wearing my sling pumps and bright colors, feeling gay inside, as if I were dancing. When the patients cheered up at the sight of me, it was applause. It was love. I gave it. And they returned it and it helped."

Changes came quickly. She wasn't afraid of being pitied now. She could walk out with a young man of an evening as gaily and confidently as any girl. The theater was over for her, but all else beckoned and she saw herself living a normal, happy and creative life.

"You'll meet John Kincey, my husband," she said. "And I want you to know about him because he had his struggles, too—another kind—and came out of them the way I did. There were ups and downs. There were mistakes. And there was fear. You never get on top of life and stay there the easy way. You have to work at it all the time. You know what terrified me? When the doctor told me I was pregnant. That was my worst scare. I don't know why. I could do wonders with one hand—but what about lifting a baby and putting it down, and changing diapers? You've seen people with two hands struggle frantically with a wriggling baby—truly—wondering if I could be a proper mother—that's what bothered me most of all.

"I had to have some help on that one and a metaphysical practitioner straightened me out. She said metaphysicians had a lot going for them because they could *talk* to their children from the first day on! Now listen to this: no matter how young, she said, babies would understand if you gave them half a chance. The idea had got around in the world that little babies didn't have intelligent response until they were three or four—well, was I going to accept that, when children were part of *consciousness?* If I affirmed it, my baby would be quiet for me whenever necessary. I would only have to make it clear that he ought to co-operate and that I needed his help, and he'd respond. The practitioner convinced me. She said we don't give children enough respect or *ask* enough *of* them. Our capacities are enormous from the time we're born; we don't half use them.

"I began to accept that I had months to practice all the

things young mothers do. Neighbors with small babies let me lift them, and stood by ready to catch. When I managed this successfully, my confidence returned.

"Tiny babies can be amazingly co-operative and intelligent. I proved it three times. Why, the first day home after the hospital, with Jeneen—the first turned out to be a girl—I said: 'Now, look here, Jeneen, I have only one arm that's working. This means you've got to help. You must lie still and not squirm.'

"If you want proof of what happened, there are neighbors still living around here who used to come and watch. Jeneen seemed to understand, and later so did the others, Allan and Desiré-Ann. If it had happened with only one, you could say the child was docile; but not one of my youngsters is docile. I expected them to meet the situation and they did. It was true of all three—and all the time. We still get along beautifully; they go to Founder's Church Sunday school, and turn to their books for ways to solve problems through affirmative prayer, just as I do. Why not? You go to the cookbook if you want to bake a special birthday cake. Well, we go to the textbook the same way. It has recipes for living and we use it every day."

Even though she was a housewife now, the doctors and therapists hadn't forgotten her. Doctors with unhappy, discouraged patients sent for her. Cars would come for her and off she'd go to make an entrance in some dreary ward, a gay testimonial to what could be accomplished even after honest medical opinion had declared: paralyzed for life. The doctors agreed with Ernest Holmes when he told the young graduate physicians: "You deal with an inner healing power and so do I!"

"At first I kept making the mistake of talking to the

patients about metaphysics," Sally continued. "But I learned. It's a funny thing—so often there's a mental barrier; as if the subject embarrassed them or they didn't want to get acquainted with God. Why is that? Because they've heard so much in their childhood that they can't believe? They thought I was a little crazy to talk about affirmative prayer, so finally I just dropped it. It's something each person has to find in his own way, at his own time—his own tough time."

One day she left the hospital a few steps behind an elderly woman who had just been discharged. Out on the busy street the lady suddenly regretted the stiff-necked pride which had kept her from confessing to the doctors that she had nowhere to go. As she waited with Sally for the light to change, she blurted out her situation—nowhere to go, and no money, either.

"That's easy," Sally said. "Come home with me."

Now here, she said, was where we would have to understand about John Kincey. He had been in the Navy—honorably discharged—was a printer and lithographer, and now was studying at UCLA on a scholarship. When she brought Mrs. Cooper home, he accepted the idea of welcoming a stranger as if the whole thing had been planned in advance. And that was only the beginning. On her trips to the hospital she kept meeting people who needed shelter for a few more days, or weeks, or months. Sometimes they could pay their way and sometimes they couldn't. "When you need help, you need help right now," Sally said.

The house could be added to—they had a big lot—so that's what happened: they kept building on extra bedrooms in their spare time. In the course of this they learned to do everything but plumbing and electrical wiring.

On the theory that any dancer who had learned book-keeping can also pick up electrical wiring, Sally bought a thirty-five-cent book at Sears, and while John and the children were sawing and hammering she sat, chin in hand, at the kitchen table storing up wisdom about electricity. She got it the same hard way she learned bookkeeping.

"Whenever you study anything, it's deeper than you expect," Sally said. "I had to pass a test and get a license. The book was baffling, so I would have to go out on the jobs where electricians worked and have them interpret things I couldn't understand. The men were always kind and helpful. On the day the tests were announced, I got downtown early—and passed.

"And now we have all these extra bedrooms and our place is called Bright View Sheltered Care Facilities. That was John's idea—Bright View. It's odd how things get carried on, the good things. I'd been talking about the Memorial Service for Dr. Ernest Holmes, and John said that Dr. Holmes' philosophy had given me the bright view that healed me, and that ought to be the name.

"I go to the church every Sunday. Here's a man gone on, a great man, and here we are with a place built with miracles, carrying on an idea I first began to understand when I was a little girl.

"I'll always remember the Memorial Service with the hundreds and hundreds of people crowded outside Founder's Church, and the traffic policemen on the corners, and the amplifiers so that folks who loved him and couldn't find seats could still hear the service and honor his memory.

"I didn't feel sad. It's very doubtful if anything dies, certainly not anything as miraculous as consciousness. I thought about all the times I'd seen him, especially the day he said I was a girl with a future. Well, he was right.

"It wasn't the way I planned in the beginning—but when we began to see what could be done here, on this big lot, by building on extra bedrooms, well, we planned then—and as soon as we started planning, the wonders happened.

"Somebody said to me, 'You've had a lot of little miracles in your life,' and I said, 'No—BIG miracles,' and that's true!"—the look on her face lit up the room. "That's how we keep this place going, with miracles—how many shelters do you find where you can be taken in no matter who you are or what's in your wallet? If we have a room and you need one, you can get in.

"And it's dramatic around here, and gay, too. Last Christmas, for instance, the patients heard about the beautiful lights downtown, between Central Avenue and Avalon in the 9000 block. The colors were just gorgeous. So we bundled everybody up—bedpans and all—and took them in relays in the station wagon. They felt better all during Christmas because they had that memory. We have a license and all but we're a little different shelter from most just as Dr. Holmes was different from most clergymen. We have fun here, there's laughter and music and hope."

The day we went to Bright View for the dedication ceremony where city officials, an assemblyman and other notables were speakers, we inspected the graceful, attractive structure with ramps for wheel chairs. There were tasteful, muted colors. We encountered cheerful patients at every turn. One elderly gentleman on crutches stood in a hall waiting for the ceremonies to begin. From a radio in a nearby bedroom came Dixieland jazz played by experts, and the patient, unaware of being watched, produced a syncopated rhythm with the thumping of his crutches while skillfully tapping the heel and toe of his good foot. We pointed him out to Sally.

"That's another reason it's Bright View," she said. "We've got the spirit of the dance around here, too."

12

The Light

"Each prophet comes to identify himself with his thought, and to esteem his hat and shoes sacred," observed Ralph Waldo Emerson. Not true of that prophet-philosopher Ernest Holmes! The gift for detachment which sometimes arrested him in mid-oratorical flight was often enough in evidence during his life and especially so—I suspect—on that last April day.

In the essay on Nature just quoted, Mr. Emerson made a further observation pertinent to this account: "No man is quite sane; each has a vein of folly in his composition, a slight determination of blood to the head, to make sure of holding him hard to one point which nature has taken to heart."

The point nature had taken to heart in Ernest's case, and to which he held hard from boyhood on, was his belief in immortality. We now will be as forthright as he was and use unmistakable language: Ernest believed in the survival of individual consciousness after death.

Painstaking investigations of psychic phenomena forced him to conclude, as we indicated earlier, that, even at their honest best, the psychics were confused and sometimes self-deluded, the most gifted seemed to be working through his own or another's consciousness. But on the contrary, the mystics, though separated by centuries, cultures and religious concepts, all sensed and taught the same truth. Illumined men and women, ages apart, went forth over the mountain to their revelations and returned with the report: we come from Life, we are in Life, we are One with Life, Life is eternal, each man will arrive at the final goal with none forgotten.

"We have nothing to fear in the universe," Ernest said, and so ordered his own life and thought.

The Law existed, had been demonstrated to exist, and would not make life meaningless at the end of one experience, on one plane.

Take this aspect of the philosophy, for example: Once the principle is understood in a universe of surpassing fruition, lack is erased to reveal ever-present abundance.

"Somewhere there is already provided a lavish abundance for every want," he said in *Science of Mind,* "a supply equal to any claim made upon it—*but the demand must be made.* Each has the power to demand his share of the gifts God has provided of health, wealth and power. Each is supplied *as* he believes."

One Sunday Ernest's car eased up to the marquee of the theater after the morning lecture. Webb, his driver, came around and opened the door. At this point a stranger separated himself from the crowd and accosted Ernest as he was about to step into the car.

"Car and chauffeur, huh?" the man said. "Quite a racket you've got, Dr. Holmes."

"On the contrary," said Ernest. "It would be a racket if I didn't have them."

Members of the congregation still lingering on the sidewalk broke into applause. The car was moving off when the caustic stranger at last closed his mouth. Somebody explained Ernest's remark in metaphysical terms, but the man was conditioned to ancient nonsense and never did understand.

In what period of mad denial of springtime's bursting beauty had mankind embraced the notion that lack, limitation, suffering and bitter sacrifice were pleasing in the eyes of a bountiful God?

Ernest's confidence in the validity of his belief in immortality was based on uncountable demonstrations of the soundness of the philosophy in other areas. He could say:

"There is something Divine about us that we have overlooked. There is more to us than we realize." He added: "But I cannot base my hopes of immortality on the revelation of anyone but myself." And then he made it explicit:

"I believe in the continuation of personal life beyond the grave, in the continuity of the individual stream of consciousness with a full recollection of itself and the ability to know and make itself known. I wish to feel, when the experience of physical death shall occur, that that which I really am will continue. I wish to feel that I shall again meet those friends whose lives and influences have made my life happy while on earth. If I could not believe this, I would believe nothing in life; life would have no meaning and death would not be untimely, unless it were long delayed. If personality does not persist beyond the grave, then death would be an event devoutly to be longed for and sought after.

"I believe that certain experiences have given us ample evidence to substantiate the claim of immortality. I know that my own experience justifies a complete acceptance of my own and other people's immortality."

Such statements, in equally explicit terms, appear in the earliest editions of his work; if nature had given him a slight "determination of blood to the head to make sure of holding him hard to one point" she certainly succeeded; only a year before that last April evening, the lonely man could be seen at his desk writing:

"Man is born of eternal day. Not because he wills it or wishes it, not because he labors or strives toward it, not because he earns it as a reward, but simply because the Spirit has breathed life into him and the Spirit which has breathed life into man cannot take it away."

On those misty spring mornings, early in April, 1960, I stopped in at the big house on Lorraine Boulevard each day on my way to the office. He had been ill—he had again "forgotten for a little while"—but the doctor said he could recover. He was tired, though. His friendly greeting came as if from some invisible departure-point. He was a traveler packed for a journey with his ticket in his hatband. When I talked about the church, and the near-capacity attendance at an early service, or the congregation's satisfaction in the structure their help and generosity had brought into being, he would respond with a shadow of the old enthusiasm—but still I had interrupted at the depot the dreams of a man whose mind already was centered on his destination.

That morning in April he was much improved. He wasn't as talkative as he had been sometimes, but he was amused at my "particular rarity" of the day before. I now brought anecdotes to him as he used to take them to Hazel. The old familiar twinkle was in his eyes when I finished my story and he looked at me for several seconds, drew breath to speak and then didn't. I wish I knew what he might have said—perhaps a triviality; perhaps not.

Ernest could accomplish more with facial expression than many another with words; wry comment was projected with a lift of the brow; rebuke with an unspoken questioning glance; and he could invite you to rethink nonsense with a half smile ending with pursed lips, arched brows and a dubious shrug. The stage lost an actor, of course; but though the inner surges that take some young men early into Hamlet were also obviously in him he was never tempted so far as I recall. Of course he would declaim poetry at the slightest provocation, always apt, sometimes sentimental. Once, with tears rolling down his cheeks, he recited a sad poem for us; at the end he dug for his handkerchief, used it mightily, apologized and said: "Now, hold on, I can do it better than that!"—and did it once again. He was right. It was better with less emotion.

It comes back to me now, the piercing look he gave me when I said, heartened by his appearance, "See you tomorrow, Ernest." I was honestly reassured. The tension had gone from the room. A nurse assured me that he was ever so much better, he had briskly laid down the law about what he would and would not eat. His tone said that he was head of the house and in complete dominion. We all thought this was the sign of recovery. I wired the news of his improvement to my fellow ministers.

About eleven-thirty that evening the call came to my home. They asked me to hurry to the Lorraine Boulevard house.

He had dropped into a peaceful sleep. The journey about which he'd been curious since his earliest investigation of the world's religions had begun almost before anyone was aware that he had gone.

As I drove away from his house in the pre-dawn darkness, his words came back:

"When the great day comes, say a few words, Bill—but keep 'em few."

I kept them few—and used some of his own. But now these years later I must say this: I've known many who have the hope of immortality, but never anyone as serenely convinced as this student of the world's philosophies. In a day when the mechanists were in ascendancy, a period when mankind had got drunk on the "little science which estranges him from God" and had not yet sobered up to the "larger science which would bring him back," in an era when the madman Hitler, and the megalomaniac Uncle Joe had become "statesmen" who scoffed at the God in the universe and made a god of the state—bringing fear and horror into the lives of millions, and death to uncounted multitudes—this man Holmes held to an Ultimate Good and was unswerving in the vision that took him beyond the headlines. In his classes at the Institute he would go to the blackboard with his chalk and with swift diagrams clarify abstract ideas so that before long his students found themselves caught up in the most engrossing enterprise anybody can engage in: the exploration of the infinitude of man, which reveals the Presence and the awareness that the infinitude within and without are nowhere separate:

One Life, One Mind, and Time with its Capital *T* yet to be properly understood.

The services were held on April 11, 1960.

In the eulogy I quoted these words which he had written long before:

"When we came into this life we were met by loving friends who cared for us until we were able to care for ourselves. Judging the future by the past and going from the known to the unknown, we can believe that when we enter the larger life there will be loving hands to greet us and loving friends to care for us until we become accustomed to our new surroundings."

He had said that he wouldn't attend the funeral—"I'll be busy elsewhere"—and he had insisted that there should be no entourage to the cemetery. But I put my family in my car as the funeral coach was driving away from the church and by chance we followed through the city streets toward the freeway. And when the time came for parting, he went one way, I another, and I said: "Godspeed, Ernest," and thus we let him go.

If there was a sense of his presence as I sat alone in the semidarkness of my study later that evening, he was in my heart, my mind, my dearest memory. He had been my mentor, friend—almost a father. He encouraged me to go to Switzerland to study with C. G. Jung; he'd had a father's pride when I served as guest chaplain in the United States Senate; he had urged me to go to Africa and visit Dr. Albert Schweitzer in his jungle hospital, which later I did. Ernest himself was happy at home. He had little interest in travel, and so if there were places and men to visit, he was content to await a report from others. He had been generous in every way, in every particular, a wise, kindly, mighty man of God—but never one to "esteem his hat and shoes sacred." He held the long view, and his gift for detachment was evident even in the organization of the Religious Science churches.

There are Religious Science churches all over this land, and in many another, where Ernest's textbooks are used and his philosophy taught by former students. But to evolve into higher understanding of the Spiritual Universe, man and church must be free. He had said this often and meant it. For years he had felt that Love, Law and Loyalty were organization enough; in practical affairs a bit more is required, but I doubt if any other similar organization places upon fellow members so few restraints or offers as many opportunities.

As I came back to the sanctuary the next morning, I paused to look at the row of gardenia bushes Ernest had ordered. Here were the grass and the flowers he had wished to see at the church entrance. I thought of the demonstrations, evidentials, Capital C Coincidences, big and little miracles—call them what you will—and knew they would continue.

He had given us techniques which carried the student ever deeper—but always in balance—into the Spiritual Universe. He taught that an *already-believing* identification with the solution would dissolve the problem; and so we, who know that these things do happen, present these last evidentials to illustrate the teaching. I believe they prove the soundness of the principle, and if this be true we can accept with the mystic's own serenity, Jesus' promise: "In my Father's house are many mansions: if it were not so, I would have told you. . . ."

Two healings in particular illuminate the theme Ernest stressed in all his writings, and which threads through this book: all you will ever need of healing Power exists now, within, in a Presence nearer than breathing, closer than hands and feet. No matter how desperate your situation, there are techniques which have been proven in cases as dire as any you may meet. Only *you* will know the wonder of finding the solution to the problem by moving into a new area of consciousness; you will discover that it sometimes is anything but easy, but the rewards are rich in compensation. Take the case which now is known to the sixteen hundred friends as *The Miracle of Mrs. Merey.* In this instance, as in Sally Kincey's story, we have used real names because the testimonials are so dramatic—to some they'll seem incredible—and because in gratitude to the philosophy these people have permitted their true names to be used in what might otherwise be an invasion of privacy.

Mrs. Merey's Miracle: The call came one morning at the office in Founder's Church. Carla and Chickie Merey, professional dancers, had been students in our Sunday school since early childhood. They were now in their late teens and had gathered enough Capital C Coincidences to turn with confidence to the Power within at a time of crisis. The doctors at the nearby hospital had told them nothing more could be done—medically—for their mother.

"The doctors say that she can't live much longer," Carla Merey told me on the phone. "They've said there's nothing to do but wait for the end."

"How do you and Chickie feel about it?"

"We just can't believe Mom's finished with us yet," Carla said.

"I'll be right there," I promised.

There were four Merey daughters, three of whom were dancers and metaphysicians. Only Carla and Chickie and Mrs. Merey were known to me. At the hospital I found other members of the family in the waiting room, including Mrs. Merey's brother, an army doctor. Carla told me that so little hope had been held out for Mrs. Merey's recovery that some of the relatives, who had obligations elsewhere, had already begun discussing funeral arrangements.

A young doctor, deeply concerned for the family, led me down the corridor toward Mrs. Merey's room. He said crushingly:

"Reverend, she's dying. Frankly, there is no hope."

"Is Mrs. Merey still alive, doctor?"

He waited with his hand at the door.

"She won't be long. She's in a coma."

"Where life is, God Is," I said.

The room was hushed except for the sound of labored breathing.

Two operations had been performed recently. In the last operation it had been necessary to remove most of her small intestine, and now Mrs. Merey was suffering from peritonitis and gangrene.

Carla and Chickie were on either side of the bed, holding their mother's hands. Another sister, Mrs. Elizabeth Rae, had flown in from San Francisco. She was in the room, standing a little to one side, not far from the nurses; she, too, was a metaphysician and had been "treating" since she arrived.

Conscious of the curious, wry glances from two nurses,

I moved up to the bed. The girls made way for me. The breathing pattern was all too familiar, shallow, rasping sounds in a tight throat; Mrs. Merey's eyes had rolled back, the hands were so cold and limp as to seem almost lifeless. I reached across to Carla, then to Chickie, and our own hands made a small circle over the bed.

"I've been praying just to keep a vigil," Chickie whispered. "To be aware. To let pass what will. But to be steadfast in our love and trust in Him as Life."

"Mother's interested in everything we do," Carla insisted. "She *must* want to stay, Dr. Hornaday."

"We will turn to the healing Power within and *believe* that Life goes on expressing Life," I told them.

No doubt the nurses suspected us of performing the last rites in some new fashion. But "there will be a new church founded on moral science," said the great Emerson, himself a mystic, and it was here. We were acting for the new church.

What can we say in cold type about a healing like this to people who do not know us? A sense of warmth and love and happy expectancy, the shining faith of young women who *knew* how to envision the solution rather than the problem; that already-believing sense of a greater Reality—this and more was with us at the bedside: prayers of affirmation demanded action and we spoke the Word.

We heard a deep, shuddering sigh. The patient began to breathe more normally. A nurse appeared at the bedside and stared in disbelief. Mrs. Merey's eyes had closed naturally and a trace of color—so little as to have been a reflection of a change within—was in her cheeks. There was a new sense of livingness about her. We exchanged glances. Our hearts had already lifted. I remember affirming:

"God's creative Power is right here, right now, and in action!"

The nurse hurried out. Soon a doctor, then another, joined us at the bed. What was happening here? they asked. We couldn't tell them. Our treatment was finished. We stepped outside.

A joyous knowledge of the ever-available law, the proof that in a universe properly understood we have nothing to fear—I know no greater thrill than such an experience. In that moment there existed before our eyes the very Glory of God.

Mrs. Merey's recovery was consistent and rapid and to the doctors, incredible. The surgeon nicknamed her Mrs. Marble-Granite and said finally when she had fully recovered:

"Whatever happened, you did it, we didn't. We did all that modern medicine could do and had reached the end of our resources."

"It was prayer," Carla told him.

"Our kind of prayer," explained Mrs. Merey, and went into detail. The doctor shrugged.

"Don't you believe in prayer?"

"I don't know."

"The change took place as soon as we all began treating properly," Chickie insisted. "Don't you believe that, ither?"

"I just don't know."

In later investigation we found that Mrs. Merey had known that she was desperately ill, but she did not fear death or think of dying. The girls still needed her. She insists that even when she was under the anesthetic, she had been aware of the doctors' grave concern. She heard their comments. She had one of those not infrequently reported hallucinations of being disembodied and somewhere in the room watching the procedure, seeing herself objectively on the table surrounded by busy doctors and nurses. This may have been a fantasy of imagination upon returning to consciousness, but, nevertheless, she remembers thinking unflattering things about her small wasted frame, gray hair and her apparent age.

"I never told the doctors about *that,* however!" she laughed. "They had too much else to try to believe as it was. They still shake their heads whenever they see me coming."

Two days before these lines were written, the doctors who had followed her medical history with amazement (and they're in for an even greater surprise if they read this) asked if she'd come again to the hospital for X rays. Two doctors were planning to write the case for a medical journal—a paper which was certain to be inconclusive, because nobody knew what happened.

The X rays turned out fine and all is well.

When we interviewed Mrs. Merey and the girls for this report, Mrs. Merey confessed:

"The dietitian, or somebody, worked out a bland diet for me which included nothing that is theoretically difficult to digest. At the head of the list, in capitals, it said: NO SPICES. Now, at our house we are very fond of refried beans and chili and enchiladas, and the last days in the hospital I was famished for Mexican food. I didn't mention this to the doctors, of course. I knew what they'd say even before I saw the diet list. On the way home in the car I could think of nothing but tacos. So we stopped and got some. How could beans and cornmeal or spices hurt me if

I didn't *believe* they'd hurt me? And I knew they wouldn't! Tacos were better than medicine for me. The taste was exactly what I needed to remind me that I was alive again. And more: I was home."

The sixteen hundred friends were not surprised when Mrs. Merey began attending the Wednesday night class again. They had treated for her, too. We do not have testimonial meetings, but anybody who has been given up for dead and comes back looking better than ever—and leaving behind her puzzled, skillful, dedicated doctors muttering: "She's made of marble-granite"—is entitled to take a bow. Granite, marble and Mrs. Merey all are part of a spiritual universe in which there are laws and laws which supersede laws; Mrs. Merey was dying under one set of laws, but a higher law was called into action—so we believe; but here again only those to whom it happens know, for a certainty, that this is true.

Let us point out in passing another side of this coin, not necessarily negative:

Once in an earlier experience a lovely gentlewoman called me to her bedside in the hospital. She was still beautiful, frail now, but with lovely bone structure and snow-white hair. She was in her late eighties. A group who adored her were in the waiting room, daughter, son-in-law, grandchildren—metaphysicians all. She begged me to persuade her family to stop praying to keep her here, and to let her go.

"I'm not trying to set any longevity records," she smiled. "I'm an old woman and I've lived too long without my husband. He and all my friends are on the other side. I'm tired. Please tell my family I love them. We all believe that life is eternal. Tell them they must let me go."

I'll never forget the round-eyed, tearful face of a pretty eight-year-old who loved her "Grandma." She was the last to say: "We'll pray for whatever is best for Grandma."

The family was left with a new understanding and no one mourned; that night, very quietly, in her sleep, Grandma slipped away.

From the day in boyhood when he read "Self-Reliance" to the evening he withdrew his consent to remaining here—and passed on naturally, and so quietly as to leave disbelief in the hushed room—Ernest Holmes worked to clarify the techniques for using the Power within under every circumstance.

The true story which follows stands high among our evidentials, Capital C Coincidences, demonstrations, answers to prayer—again choose as you will—as an illustration of what can happen when a man extends himself and in his extremity discovers the Power within.

Jed Emery Hudson, a cardiac patient, a man in his late fifties, lived alone on a small desert ranch near Barstow, California. I was eyewitness to what happened on the evening of the day after the most desperate night of his life.

He lay in his bedroom near midnight, listening to a radio talk on station KFI, Los Angeles—listening, not because he was interested, but because he hesitated to lift his arm to turn off the transistor.

He couldn't forget that his own doctor had brought a specialist to examine him. Afterward there had been headshaking and a quiet consultation in another room. He couldn't hear what they said, but he didn't need to. He was told not to move more than necessary, not even to shave.

They needn't have worried. When he did move, even to turn over, he was instantly aware of a skittering, faulty heartbeat. The last cardiogram was what had brought the specialist. He had urged Jed to let them call the ambulance and move him to the hospital in town. Jed flatly refused. He couldn't afford it. They offered to send him to the county hospital. Jed said the trip would kill him. But it was criminal negligence, they felt, to leave a man in the ranchhouse alone without a phone, ministered to only by the neighbors and a county nurse who came on schedule but not often enough.

He dismissed them.

He'd made up his mind to "tough it out" with the help of the neighbor's boy Petey. He would die right here. He had willed the ranchhouse and his land to a much-beloved daughter in the East.

They had lingered, urging him to send for his daughter. But she had four children under eight—grandchildren he had never seen—and she couldn't get away, he said. It was better not to worry her. When she inherited the ranch it would help out and he enjoyed thinking about that. All he wanted was to go easy in his sleep and avoid suffering.

They left him a new box of heart pills and a few sedatives. Then his own doctor said good-by too quickly, amended it to, "So long, fella," and both went out.

Jed didn't need any more medical opinion than he'd been able to get out of the atmosphere.

At dusk the neighbor's wife brought a bowl of chicken soup. Jed wasn't hungry, but he tried to spoon up some of it to please her. The neighbors lived on the adjoining quarter section and shared a well with him and couldn't have been kinder. Their house was some seventy yards away and Petey, their son, a Boy Scout, had built an ingenious signal device for Jed: a pole which slanted upward from the bedroom window and leaned against a cross-T out in the clothesyard. One end of a cord on a pulley had been pinned to the bed sheet within easy reach. Jed could get fast service when he moved his fingers and inched a flour sack aloft. Sometimes a phone would have been no quicker. Petey, keeping a vigil at his own windows, came running when needed. Nothing was too much trouble for Petey. And also, as he remarked one day, up to now he'd never seen a dead man. And there was a kid in his patrol who had.

The manner of Petey's arrival rarely varied and was not reassuring. Whenever the flour sack rippled in the breeze, Jed could hear thick-soled tennis shoes pounding across the sand: then the thudding arrival would be followed by a long uneasy silence. Presently, a bristling crew-cut would appear above the sill, followed by a worried young brow and finally Petey's anxious eyes.

"Hi-ya, Mr. Hudson," he'd say huskily. "Gettin' any worse?"

You didn't need more than this to figure out what Petey's family thought the chances were. But that didn't matter. Jed himself had known how serious the attack was in the first smashing blow which had sent him to his knees in the barn.

Now, as the radio voice filled the darkened room, Jed's fingers inched toward the transistor on the bed beside him; he had reached the knob when a phrase arrested his attention:

"Is there anyone listening to my voice who is in difficulty —ill—miserable—fearful. . . . ?"

This was the program called *This Thing Called Life* which Ernest Holmes had turned over to me many years before.

That particular midnight the script had been inspired by the Nobel Prize winner we have mentioned earlier. Dr. Alexis Carrel had published his famous *Man, the Unknown,* a book of which Will Durant said: "The wisest, profoundest, most valuable book that I have come upon in the American literature of our century."

Dr. Carrel insisted that man can become the actual ruler of his universe. Though Carrel himself was a famous doctor, the book courageously disregarded many accepted medical beliefs. It had been a best-seller when first published. I'd always kept a copy, paperback or otherwise, around the house, and one turned up on my desk the evening I worked on that particular group of radio scripts. The original edition had been published in 1935; there had been fifty-five printings in the hard-cover edition, and the book had been translated into eighteen foreign languages. Perhaps years had passed since it had last been mentioned on the air; but its message wasn't dated—the Truth doesn't grow old. A footnote on page 101 suggested a sermon idea: Dr. Carrel confessed that he had been investigating metaphysical healing since 1902. And secretly, in the beginning—never daring, in those early years, to mention to another doctor what he was up to.

"The investigation of such phenomena is still more delicate than that of telepathy and clairvoyance," he had written. "But science has to explore the entire field of reality."

It would have been dangerous to his career if he admitted publicly an interest in this mode of healing, whereas, today, any physician may openly observe the patients who are brought to Lourdes and many other shrines. Many physicians are puzzled by the seeming "miracles" that sometimes occur. And there are those who are keeping careful records.

"Lourdes is the center of an International Medical Association, composed of many members. There is a slowly growing literature about miraculous healing," he wrote. "The only condition indispensable to the occurrence of the phenomenon is prayer. But there is no need for the patient himself to pray, or even to have any religious faith. It is sufficient that someone around him be in a state of prayer."

Of course, at Lourdes, as at other shrines, not everyone is healed. Perhaps only a few. But the healings which have been witnessed and attested to would indicate that a *law,* little known to mankind, is in operation. In the metaphysical movement we know this to be true; we have a constant flow of testimony; but few of us have medical records of the sort filed by the Medical Bureau of Lourdes.

Dr. Carrel pointed out: "Our present conception of the influence of prayer upon pathological lesions is based upon the observation of patients who have been cured almost instantaneously of various affections, such as peritoneal tuberculosis, cold abscesses, osteitis, suppurating wounds, lupus, cancer, etc. The process of healing changes little from one individual to another. Often, an acute pain. Then a sudden sensation of being cured."

That a man of Dr. Carrel's standing would subscribe to such material was, of course, sensational. The healings brought about by Jesus and his followers in the first few centuries of the young Christian church to many people were now merely legendary. However, eyewitnesses and metaphysical practitioners believed that such healings had once taken place, were still possible, and were now being accomplished.

I pointed out in the broadcast that we had no objection whatever to calling the doctor, that all true advances made by man are useful to other men. If a pill will help, take it. If a doctor can assist, bless and use his skill. But when medicine abandons all hope, there is another Way.

Skeptics say: "The miracles of Jesus? You know what word-of-mouth can do to a story. Call them parables; maybe there's a spiritual truth hidden away in the myth." That, in my own youth, was the general attitude. It wasn't until the metaphysician came along and insisted: "No! There is LAW in action here!" that those truly trying to "follow in His steps" were supported in their hope that the so-called legends of healing occurring in the Bible stories were, actually, historical reports which illustrated the working of an eternal principle.

Why, imagine!—my broadcast said—Here was a great scientist saying, after thorough study of eyewitnessed medical testimony, that *"the only condition indispensable to the occurrence of the phenomenon is prayer!"*

"Well, then, what kind of prayer?" I asked the question in that midnight talk. "A prayer of supplication or a prayer of affirmation? Well, almost certainly it would be a prayer in which those praying envision healing and see it accomplished—see the solution, not the problem."

I said: "The answer to any prayer is in the prayer when prayed. That is why the greatest Teacher who ever lived said, 'all things are possible to him that believeth.' Now, if there is anyone listening to my voice who has given up

—know with me that you, right now, can do something about it. Whatever your problem is, it is an idea in your mind. Change the idea and you can change the effect. With God there is no great or small, and where you are, God Is. Remember, it is done unto you as you believe. So check your belief. If you believe that a change for the better is now taking place—if you *really* believe it—it will occur. You can count on it."

Earlier, Jed Emery Hudson, with his room drenched in music followed by even louder commercials had been trying not to count his heartbeat. Ever since the doctors' visit he had been more sharply aware of the pulse in his throat, the uneven hammering in his chest. There had been an air of finality in that "So long"; worst of all had been their effort to be cheerful, to hide what they really felt. Jed couldn't stop thinking about them and now, as midnight approached and Petey and the neighbors were sleeping, the loneliness closed in and he was as desperate as a man can be.

But the words on the radio had come intact into the room and seemed to linger above the bed.

Into his terror had come a man's voice talking calmly about a famous scientist who attested to recorded cases of metaphysical healing. Healing! Jed's mind caught up a reference to affirmative prayer and the suggestion that one's mind could actually heal, that all mankind may turn to an ever-available Power within. Well, why not? What did he have to lose? When he heard the name at the end of the program he burned it into his mind: pronounced it with an *"e,"* "Dr. Hornadee."

As the night wore on, he kept repeating in his thoughts: *"All things are possible to him that believeth. If I really believe a change for the better is taking place, I can count on it. I can count on it."*

With unrhythmic heartbeats shaking his body, he felt for the cord and then, resting after each small exertion, pulled his flour sack into the wind. He could hear only the dry, brittle sound of its snapping in the darkness. He lay back and, presently, fell asleep. When he awakened, it was morning, and he was frightened. Why had no one come? But then he heard the pounding of Petey's sneakers and soon was conscious of Petey's eyes.

"Mr. Hudson," the boy whispered loudly, "you still okay?"

"Phone!" gasped Jed. "Get your daddy. Tell him to bring the truck. I gotta get in town. Got to phone a man—got to get to Los Angeles."

"Los Angeles!" the boy said, horrified. "You'll never make it."

"I ain't makin' it here, either," Jed repeated weakly. "Hurry, boy. Get your dad."

Petey ran.

The excitement gave Jed the strength to reach for his shirt, and after a while, his pants. When the wondering neighbors finally arrived with the pickup truck, they found Jed dressed except for his shoes. Petey knelt down and helped. They all expected him to die before they carried him outdoors.

"You're too sick," they protested. "You're never gonna make it, Jed."

"I sure wasn't makin' it last night," he said. "I was dyin' alone. I'd rather die outside, anyhow."

They managed an inch at a time to get him down the steps.

He whispered, "Get me to where I can call Dr. Hornadee."

Reluctantly they lifted him into the truck. He lay gasping while Petey held him up and tried to give him a sip of water from his Scout canteen.

They drove off gently.

Near a gas station on the outskirts of Barstow, they stopped at a roadside phone booth and carried Jed toward it, a few steps at a time. Inside, he clung to the phone for a few minutes and then placed a person-to-person call to "Dr. Hornadee" at KFI in Los Angeles. The operator at the studio sensed his desperation and the call was transferred to the office at Founder's Church. Urgency was communicated to Georgia, my secretary, and the long-distance caller was put through.

Jed's breathing sounded like a bad attack of asthma. I told him to take his time. To calm down. From his conversation I gathered only that he feared he was dying and wanted me to pray with him.

"I'm coming in to see you," he whispered huskily. "I gotta wait for a bus outa Barstow, and I gotta change a coupla times, Dr. Hornadee. I missed the Express. It might be hours before I get there. Be late afternoon."

"I'll wait for you," I promised.

"I don't like to put you out—I might die on the way," he said, "so if I ain't there by—"

I was disturbed.

"Now look here. If you don't think you're well enough to reach Los Angeles, you shouldn't start, Mr. Hudson. Perhaps we can discuss your problem on the phone right now."

"No! No! No! I gotta see you. And when I get there, you gotta pray for me. It's my only chance."

"All right. Know that your trip will be made safely. Be affirmative. Remember, you have a Power within that stands ready to help you."

"Okay, Dr. Hornadee. I'm on my way."

He fumbled the receiver and hung up.

For me, the morning went zipping along; parades of visitors, phone calls, a conference, a discussion with the architect about plans for the new chapel, travel arrangements for our lecture trip to Japan—nothing more could have been squeezed into that day. By evening, when I was washing up, more than ready for home, Georgia reminded me of a sick man inward bound from the desert. Just then a girl at KFI called to remind me that my scripts for tomorrow's taping session had not been mimeographed. There was a good reason: they hadn't been written. I pulled up a yellow pad and went to work. The office staff, one by one, bade me good night. I phoned home to announce that I'd be late for dinner.

"How late, do you think, Bill?" my wife asked.

"Surely not very late," I said.

I went out into the meditation garden and studied Ernest's tree, gave it silent admiration, patted the trunk with an approving hand. Then I found myself wondering if the other trees were disturbed emotionally because so much attention went to the one in the middle. They weren't growing as fast, and that was a fact. So the others were duly blessed and I sensed a "Thank you." It was cool in the garden, with the fresh damp fern fragrance; crystal drops from the spray clung to leaves. It's a small garden but it's restful to step into; a breath of woodland. Ernest had been fond of it.

Quiet settled down. It was six-twenty when a door banged, somewhere far away at the Sixth Street side, and I heard running footsteps growing louder in the corridor. An echoing voice boomed.

"Dr. Hornadee! He-e-e-e-y, *Dr. Hornadee!*"

Then Jed Emery Hudson, wild of eye, stood in my doorway and began to jump up and down, hammering his chest with a clenched fist.

"Look at me!" he roared, running in position, lifting his knees high. *"You healed me. You healed me!"* He jumped up and down. "I haven't felt this good in twenty-seven years! Feel my heart! You sure prayed! Man, you sure *prayed."*

He grabbed my hand and thrust it against his shirt. There was a good heartbeat, all right.

"You did it—you did it—you did it—thank you, Doctor!"

It was a weird and wonderful scene. He danced around the office like a madman. It was some moments before I could calm him down.

"Now, hold on," I shouted. "Why, I didn't heal you, man! I didn't even pray for you."

That reached him. He stared at me.

"You didn't—what?"

"When you phoned," I explained, "you didn't tell me what your trouble was, except that you were afraid and wanted me to pray *when you got here."*

Incredulously he lowered himself into a chair. He wasn't even breathing hard.

"Then what did it?"

"Whatever it was, you did it."

"But, Doctor—I was dying. And now I'm alive. I'm better than alive. I'm the best I've been in twenty-seven years!" He was a once-rugged man—thin, wiry, sunburned, tough.

I went back to my own chair.

"Tell me about your trip to town," I suggested. "What were you thinking as you traveled along, Mr. Hudson?"

"Jed," he suggested warmly. "If anybody's got a right to call me Jed, you have, Dr. Hornadee."

But then he remembered I hadn't done anything.

"I just can't understand it," he said.

"Let's trace back," I suggested.

When finally he traced back over the trip, he decided that somewhere the other side of San Bernardino he had been astonished to find himself still alive. In a dark corner of his mind he had been prepared to die on the bus. That had seemed preferable to death in a lonely room.

He had taken a seat near the door—so as not to trouble the driver too much if he had to carry off the body. He braced his feet and held himself upright, keeping alive from minute to minute. Finally, looking out the window at the sand hills and yucca, he thought: "That fella is really bearin' down, praying." He felt distinctly better. He pictured a robed figure kneeling at an altar with candles burning. The very idea warmed his heart. Nobody had paid much attention to him lately, except Petey, the tenderfoot Scout who was doing his good deed while expecting the worst. Riding along that way in the bus it was comforting to think of a kindly old ecclesiastic, a total stranger, devoting his day to this ancient kind of healing work. It was a very Christian thing for a man to do. He was touched. Waves of gratitude washed over him, and tears came to his eyes. "God bless Dr. Hornadee," he said, and sort of dozed off.

Now, he hadn't been much of a fella for church. In fact, he hadn't been in a church since his folks made him go to Sunday school when he was seven. He wasn't mad at God, exactly; he had been more, well, indifferent-like up to now. Sometimes at Easter and Christmas and Thanksgiving —in a good year—he'd felt kind of guilty and neglectful, but never guilty enough, actually, to get dressed up and go. He meant well. He had given Petey a contribution once for the Scout troop, but that was all.

When the bus rolled through the outskirts of San Bernardino, he roused again, surprised to find himself still alive. He said a prayer of his own.

"Thank Ye, Father, for keepin' my heart goin' as far as San Bernardino."

He sat with his head bowed, eyes shut and thought deeply, trying to generate power within.

"And if Ye see fit to keep me alive on the next leg o' the trip until I get to Dr. Hornadee, I'll thank Ye for that, too. Amen."

It was not even a prayer of affirmation. There was gratitude in it, yes, and hope. And faith—in a measure. He now began to believe that God's attention had been attracted by the kindly old minister who was doing the work at his altar with the candles.

When the bus stopped next time, Jed waited until the passengers got out and then he made his way slowly down the steps. He wasn't thinking about his heart so much now: he was beginning to feel hungry. For about four weeks he hadn't been able to eat anything but sliced chicken and soup, but now he went to the counter and ordered a hot roast beef sandwich with mashed potatoes and gravy.

It was very tasty. It was mellow, day-old gravy, the best kind. He ate everything on his plate.

Then there was a long wait for the Los Angeles bus, so he leaned against an adobe wall in the shade and practiced breathing. He didn't count his pulse—didn't dare—but he was pretty sure now that he was much better.

What a minister! What a prayer!

When the bus left San Bernardino, the phrase he had been repeating since last night came sweeping back in cadence with the passing telephone poles: *If I really believe a change for the better is taking place, I can count on it. I can count on it. I can count on it.* He kept saying this and counting, and with the swift passing of every tenth pole he decided he was actually getting well. It was a miracle. Ten more and another ten, better, a little better, better, a little better. A sense of joyous health swept over him from deep inside. Just before they reached Los Angeles he realized with an absolute certainty that he could run. He was tearful with gratitude.

"That old prayin' vicar is a *powerhouse!*" he thought. "He's a *saint!*"

Everything grew brighter inside and out.

Then he'd remembered his boyhood on the ranch.

In boyhood there's nary an ache nor pain—there's no *body,* hardly. There's a wild spirit within a boy somewhere but no *body* until, of course, he skins a knuckle or bangs a knee. But mostly, he's just a happy, moving spirit in love with life. He wondered. Had he got all that back, too—the health of boyhood?

He was still wondering as he sat there in my office.

"Why, pretty soon, Dr. Hornadee, I began to feel frisky. I could hardly think back to when I ever felt better in my whole life."

When the bus arrived at the Los Angeles terminal, he had moved easily down the aisle with the other passengers. Some folks had thought he was plumb crazy because as soon as he got to the sidewalk he tried running in position, lifting his knees high, hammering his chest, testing. It didn't kill him, by golly! Didn't hurt him even. Made him *feel* good, in fact.

"I was dying," he explained to a group of flabbergasted passengers. "But now I'm healed." He went on exercising. "There's a pastor prayin' for me out on Sixth Street."

The people turned away, embarrassed. They thought he was off his rocker, and he was a little maybe—with pure joy. He didn't care. He saw a Sixth Street bus and hailed it.

And now, in my office, staring at me, he at last understood—and was frightened.

"I did it my own self?" he marveled. "How could I, Dr. Hornadee? I ain't even religious. Ask my neighbors—they can tell you. I've got cardiograms shootin' off the page. That little kid Petey, every time he peeked in the window he expected he'd find me cooled. How could *I* do it?"

"You saw the solution—not the problem," I explained. "Don't you understand? You were *convinced* that you'd be healed, so you released the healing Power within. You affirmed it with every passing phone pole. You affirmed it when you pictured your boyhood, and good health. You affirmed it with the word 'frisky' which I haven't heard anywhere lately. You affirmed it when you got off the bus and began to hammer your chest. You were sure. You absolutely knew. *You* did it."

He held both hands to his head for a moment.

"Do you suppose the same thing happens to those folks at Lourdes?"

"Yes, I believe so. There is a *law* in operation here. We keep learning more about it. And when scientific genius in the universities decides to explore the spiritual universe unhampered by either dogma or cynicism, there'll be other great discoveries. But this much you and I know for sure as of tonight: the law has operated for you. We may not be able to convince anybody else of this, but *we know* it. Your neighbors will be impressed, but they'll discount all this. They'll decide that most of your trouble was imagination. Your doctor, no doubt, will show the cardiograms at a medical meeting and the learned man will conclude that you were in an hysterical condition which affected your heart. Only you know that whereas you were desperate, dying, now you are free. Others may call it a coincidence."

"Yeah," he said slowly, "I *thought* you were praying for me, so I got well. It's a coincidence all right."

"Coincidence with a capital C, Jed," I suggested, "but also a capital G. God's in it. He has to be. He has to be in everything."

Jed Emery Hudson's Christmas card turns up each year along with a personal message. The last one reads: *Heart fine. Doing land developing. If you ever want a desert hideaway, let me know. Still think about that great day in your office.*

His card is delivered to my office at the church in mid-December and is addressed to Dr. Hornadee.

* * *

It was remarkable—but then! What wonders we take for granted every morning and evening, every spring, every fall. We have the cleansing snows of winter, the rain in season, the thrust of seed in soil. When love is tarnished or beauty destroyed, the fault is easily determined and is not God's. We have been given such beauty as to put us on our knees in gratitude. Our streams were clean, our skies were clean, our countryside quiet and fruitful under a benign sun—whatever has been lost of this has been marred by man unawakened; and if in his foolishness he destroys it, and himself leaves the scene, Love and Law will in due time repair his depredations and re-create the beauty and the wonder and the miracles again. But such need not be if we recognize that there is One Life—and that within each of us is the Power through which the world shall be healed. There awaits, when we understand it, all that we were given "in the beginning," Love, Truth, Beauty and Wisdom, the Presence, the living Spirit of God.

Emerson, speaking of the Infinitude of Private man, said:

"In yourself is the Law of all nature . . . in yourself slumbers the whole of Reason; it is for you to know it all; it is for you to dare all."

And our modern philosopher, Ernest Holmes, wrote in the verse which opens his textbook:

Peace be unto thee, stranger, enter and be not afraid.
I have left the gate open and thou art welcome in my home.
There is room in my house for all.
I have swept the hearth and lighted the fire.
The room is warm and cheerful and you will find comfort
and rest within.
The table is laid and the fruits of Life spread before thee.

The wine is here also, it sparkles in the light.
I have set a chair for you where the sunbeams dance through the shade.
Sit and rest and refresh your soul.
Eat of the fruit and drink the wine.
All, all is yours, and you are welcome.

And for all this, the biblical source is St. John 1:1-5,9.

In the beginning was the Word, and the Word was with God, and the Word was God.

The same was in the beginning with God.

All things were made by him; and without him was not anything made that was made.

In him was life; and the life was the light of men.

And the light shineth in darkness; and the darkness comprehended it not.

That was the true light which lighteth every man that cometh into the world.

Many centuries ago, in cottages and palaces and in caravans along the highways, a folktale was told to the children. The origin of *Aladdin and the Wonderful Lamp* cannot be traced; plot and incident varied from generation to generation, but the central idea persisted through the ages.

Beneath the story's wordliness and extravagance lay a theme which children recognized, loved and remembered. Why, look here!—the story said—even the ne'er-do-well Aladdin discovered that the magic of his name—this alone—would open the door to hidden riches. Even a heedless, disobedient boy was not denied the greatest imaginable gift: a tarnished lamp which, when rubbed to brightness, produced his heart's desire.

Was an essential truth conveyed in this long-surviving fiction?

In the seminar at Asilomar we agreed with our friend and mentor: prayer is not Aladdin's lamp. But now we have sought through a metaphysical interpretation of an ancient myth to illuminate an abstract idea for the curious, or the skeptic. Convinced metaphysicians sometimes find it difficult to communicate such ideas to puzzled friends. "What *is* it you metaphysicians actually believe?" the skeptic asks—and often enough his eyes glaze over as you try to answer.

It's rarely wise to attempt to put it into specific terms. "There's an essay by Ernest Holmes . . ." we'll say vaguely; and if they really want to know, they'll say, "Which one, and where?"

And that's where we'll leave it.

Ernest Holmes' philosophy insisted, and demonstration proved, that we can know peace of mind, health, abundance, and growth in spiritual understanding by turning with an already-believing faith to the Power within, the Divine I Am, the Light that Lighteth every man who cometh into the world.

A Shining Path awaits each of us, Ernest said—and those who seek will find it.

Sources

Carrel, Alexis. *Man, the Unknown*. New York; Harper & Bros. 1935.

Emerson, Ralph Waldo. *The Conduct of Life*. Essay on Worship.

Emerson, Ralph Waldo. Essay on Nature. Essay on Self-Reliance.

Franklin, Benjamin. *Ben Franklin's Wit and Wisdom*. Mt. Vernon; Peter Pauper Press.

Holmes, Ernest. *Creative Mind and Success*. New York; Robert M. McBride & Co. 1919.

Holmes, Ernest and Hornaday, William H. D. *Help for Today*. New York; Dodd, Mead & Co., Inc. 1958.

Holmes, Ernest. *How to Use the Science of Mind*. New York; Dodd, Mead & Co., Inc. 1950.

Holmes, Ernest. *The Science of Mind*. New York; Dodd, Mead & Co., Inc. 1938.

Holmes, Ernest. *Ernest Holmes Seminar Lectures*. Edited by Georgia C. Maxwell. League of Religious Science Practitioners, 3251 West Sixth Street, Los Angeles, California.

Iolmes, Ernest. *What Religious Science Teaches*. Church of Religious Science. 1944.

Iolmes, Ernest. Taped church dedication lectures by Ernest Holmes. Paraphrasing from Ernest Holmes tape recordings.

'riestley, J. B. *Midnight on the Desert*. New York; Harper & Bros. 1937.

'alues. University of Chicago Press. 1932.

Dr. William H. D. Hornaday was a personal friend and professional associate of Ernest Holmes for many years. He is the author or co-author of several books, including *Help For Today* (with Ernest Holmes), and he is presently the minister of Founder's Church of Religious Science in Los Angeles, one of the world's largest metaphysical churches.

The late Harlan Ware was also a friend of Ernest Holmes. As a professional writer, he had short stories published in numerous popular magazines, he wrote three novels (one of which was made into a motion picture), and for over a dozen years he was associated with the classic radio program, *One Man's Family*.